Microsoft Azure
Fundamentals

Study Guide & Exam Prep

Paul Reynolds

ISBN: 978-1-911064-15-2

Published by Black Chili Limited

For more information, please email
publications@blackchili.co.uk

Microsoft Azure Fundamentals AZ-900 - Study Guide & Exam Prep

INTRODUCTION 1

ABOUT THE AUTHOR 3
AZ-900 AZURE FUNDAMENTALS 7

EXAM OBJECTIVE 1 – CLOUD CONCEPTS 9

WHAT IS CLOUD COMPUTING? 9
CLOUD CHARACTERISTICS 11
HOW CLOUD COMPANIES DO IT 15
CAPEX VS OPEX 16
AZURE PRICING – CONSUMPTION MODELS 19
IAAS, PAAS & SAAS 21
CLOUD DEPLOYMENT MODELS 23

EXAM OBJECTIVE 2 – AZURE CORE SERVICES 27

GEOGRAPHIES, REGIONS & AVAILABILITY ZONES 27
THE DATA CENTRE 29
REGIONS 29
AVAILABILITY ZONES 30
REGION PAIRS 32
GEOGRAPHIES 33
AZURE RESOURCES 35
RESOURCE GROUPS 36
AZURE RESOURCE MANAGER 38
AZURE COMPUTE SERVICES 39
VIRTUALISATION 39
AZURE VIRTUAL MACHINES 41
AZURE VIRTUAL MACHINE SCALE SETS 42
CONTAINERS 43
AZURE CONTAINER INSTANCES 44
KUBERNETES 45

App Service 46
Azure Functions... 47
Azure Compute Summary 48
Azure Networking **51**
Azure Virtual Networks 51
VPN Gateway 53
Azure Load Balancer.................................... 53
Application Gateway 54
Content Delivery Networks 55
Azure Networking Summary 56
Azure Storage **57**
Azure Blob Storage...................................... 58
Azure Queue Storage 59
Azure Table Storage 59
Azure File Storage 60
Azure Storage Account 61
Azure Disk Storage....................................... 62
Azure Database Services **63**
Azure Cosmos DB... 64
Azure SQL Database 65
Azure SQL 66
Azure Database Services Summary............... 67
The Azure Marketplace............................. **69**
Azure IoT.. **69**
Azure IoT Hub 70
Axure IoT Central 71
Azure Sphere 71
Azure IoT Services Summary 72
Azure Big Data and Analytics **73**
Azure Synapse Analytics 74
Azure HDInsight... 75
Azure Databricks.. 75
Azure Big Data Summary.............................. 76
Artificial Intelligence (AI) on Azure **77**
Azure Machine Learning 77
Azure Machine Learning Studio 78
Azure Machine Learning Summary 79

AZURE SERVERLESS COMPUTING 81
AZURE FUNCTIONS... 81
AZURE LOGIC APPS 82
EVENT GRID... 83
AZURE SERVERLESS SUMMARY 83
AZURE DEVOPS 85
AZURE DEVOPS.. 85
AZURE DEVTEST LABS.. 86
AZURE DEVOPS SERVICE SUMMARY 87
AZURE MANAGEMENT TOOLS....................................... 89
AZURE PORTAL... 89
AZURE POWERSHELL 90
AZURE CLI.. 91
AZURE CLOUD SHELL 91
AZURE MANAGEMENT TOOLS SUMMARY............................. 92
AZURE ADVISOR... 95

EXAM OBJECTIVE 3 – SECURITY, PRIVACY, COMPLIANCE
& TRUST IN AZURE 97

AZURE SECURITY GROUPS.. 97
NETWORK SECURITY GROUPS 97
APPLICATION SECURITY GROUPS 100
AZURE SECURITY GROUPS SUMMARY 100
USER DEFINED ROUTING 101
AZURE FIREWALL 103
AZURE DDOS PROTECTION... 103
AZURE IDENTITY SERVICES 105
IDENTITY 105
AUTHENTICATION 105
AUTHORISATION.. 106
ACCESS MANAGEMENT.. 106
AZURE ACTIVE DIRECTORY... 106
MULTI-FACTOR AUTHENTICATION 107
AZURE SECURITY CENTER.. 109
AZURE KEY VAULT 111
ROLE-BASED ACCESS CONTROL 113

AZURE RESOURCE LOCKS 115
AZURE RESOURCE TAGS 117
AZURE POLICY 119
AZURE BLUEPRINTS 121
CLOUD ADOPTION FRAMEWORK 123
WHAT IS CLOUD ADOPTION? 123
PHASE 1 – STRATEGY 123
PHASE 2 – PLAN 125
PHASE 3 – READY 126
PHASE 4 – ADOPT 127
GOVERN AND MANAGE 129
SECURITY, PRIVACY AND COMPLIANCE – CORE TENETS 131
PRIVACY STATEMENT 131
ONLINE SERVICES TERMS (OST) 131
DATA PROTECTION ADDENDUM (DPA) 132
TRUST CENTER 132
AZURE COMPLIANCE DOCUMENTATION 133
AZURE SOVEREIGN REGIONS 133

EXAM OBJECTIVE 4 – AZURE PRICING, SERVICE LEVEL
AGREEMENTS AND SUPPORT 135

AZURE PRICING 135
AZURE ACCOUNT SUBSCRIPTIONS 136
BUYING AZURE SERVICES 137
HOW IS THE COST CALCULATED? 139
USAGE 140
LOCATION 140
BANDWIDTH & ZONES 141
ESTIMATING COST 141
COST REDUCTION METHODS 143
THE TCO CALCULATOR 143
AZURE ADVISOR 144
SPENDING LIMITS 144
AZURE RESERVATIONS 145
COST MANAGEMENT & BILLING CONTROL 146
ADD RESOURCE TAGS 146

REVIEW VMS 147

DELETE UNUSED RESOURCES 147

MIGRATE FROM IAAS TO PAAS 148

REDUCE LICENSING COSTS 148

AZURE COST MANAGEMENT 151

USING COST ANALYSIS 152

CUSTOMISED VIEWS 153

SAVING AND SHARING 153

BUDGETS AND ALERTS 155

ACTION GROUPS 155

COST ALERTS 155

AZURE SERVICE LEVEL AGREEMENTS 157

HOW PERCENTAGES MAP TO DOWNTIME 158

SERVICE CREDITS 158

HOW ARE OUTAGES IDENTIFIED? 159

REQUESTING SERVICE CREDITS 159

DESIGNING YOUR APPLICATION 161

THE AZURE SERVICE LIFECYCLE 163

GOOD LUCK! 165

CONTACTING THE AUTHOR 167

Introduction

Cloud computing has completely transformed the technology landscape, in what seems like a heartbeat. This guide is designed for readers with a general awareness of IT infrastructure concepts and Microsoft Azure, without specific knowledge or experience. It assumes you are preparing for a beginner-level exam – namely Microsoft Azure Fundamentals AZ-900, though it is also a good introduction to Microsoft Azure for readers not intending to sit an exam. This guide assumes no prior knowledge of Microsoft Azure.

The contents of this book were built by the author from his journey in passing the related exam.

Cloud Computing is the delivery of computing services such as servers, storage, databases, networking, software, analytics, intelligence, and more, by service providers in remote locations over the Internet.

Cloud Computing provides an alternative to the traditional datacentre. If you own or operate a datacentre, everything needs to be managed – the premises, power, cooling, purchasing, and installing hardware, virtualisation, installing the operating system, and any applications, setting up the networking, routing and network security, and data storage. You are then responsible for the full lifecycle – all the maintenance and eventual decommissioning.

But if we choose Cloud Computing, a third-party cloud vendor is responsible for datacentre operations. They also provide a wide variety of servers, software, storage, and platform as a service options. We consume whatever services we wish and are typically charged based on usage.

In the following pages you will find everything the author collated in his study of AZ-900: Microsoft Azure Fundamentals, to gain Microsoft Certification by passing the associated exam. This is a foundation level qualification, and no familiarity with Microsoft Azure is expected. Appreciation of common IT infrastructure concepts is helpful, and access to the Azure Portal via a free account will help familiarise you with the layout, giving valuable insight for the exam.

The AZ-900 examination has no pre-requisites, and you should find the material in this book sufficient to pass the AZ-900 exam. New Azure services are added frequently, so whilst this book was comprehensive at the point of going to print, please check for updates to the exam syllabus.

About the Author

I left University with an English Literature degree and like most people with English degrees who have no inclination to go into teaching; I had no idea what I was going to do. I fell into a resourcing job for a recruitment company... calling people and talking to them on the phone about technology jobs I did not understand, and getting paid minimum wage. I have that terrible job to thank for setting my future direction.

My last day at that company started uneventfully enough, until one of the many people I called that day unwittingly showed me the light. He was pretty horrible actually – I had called him regarding a contract that was obviously some way beneath him. He was direct, to put it mildly – and his parting words were, 'So you can update your records, I wouldn't take a permanent role for less than £250K'. **Two hundred and fifty *thousand* pounds?** (and this was in 1999!) At the rate I was going that would be 25 years' wages. And that was my light bulb moment.

I looked at the skills required for some of the serious consultancy roles, I was spending my days trying to fill, then researched what the jobs that fed those sorts of positions were. Having followed my nose to the entry level of the field, I set about acquiring the skills required to get through the door. I worked my way through the ranks in several jobs, which at the time I did not much appreciate, all of which allowed me to build solid experience with some of the biggest companies in the world.

I studied for professional qualifications on my own time, self-funding courses and exams – investing in myself. I have been Microsoft Certified since 1999, on Windows NT4!

My Microsoft Certifications include:

Microsoft Certified Azure Architect Expert
Microsoft Certified Azure Security Engineer
Microsoft Certified Azure Administrator
Microsoft Certified Systems Engineer
Microsoft Certified Administrator
Microsoft Certified Professional

I also hold certifications from Amazon, Novell, Forcepoint and TOGAF, amongst others.

Certifications have helped me secure ever-more senior positions in large companies and have seen my annual salary increase many times over since I started on the certification trail in 1999. All my cloud certifications have been gained without classroom teaching, using Microsoft Learn content, and other material freely available on the Internet.

Access to, and familiarity with, the Azure Portal and CLI will be a massive advantage as you approach the exam.

You will find my professional profile on LinkedIn here:

https://www.linkedin.com/in/renhimself/

AZ-900 Azure Fundamentals

This book is designed for readers who are beginning their journey in cloud computing, or looking to build on their skills in Amazon AWS or Google GCP and upgrade their existing vocabulary with that of Microsoft Azure.

There are no pre-requisites for Microsoft Azure Fundamentals AZ-900, so this book will take you from zero knowledge to being cloud-literate enough to pass the foundation exam. As the Azure Fundamentals exam is beginner level, there will be no 'deep-dive' into specific technologies, this is an introduction to core cloud computing concepts, and an overview of the Microsoft Azure services and product sets.

This book covers the four high-level areas required for the exam; the percentage of exam focused on each area is also shown below:

- Describe cloud concepts (15-20%)
- Describe core Azure services (30-35%)
- Describe security, privacy, compliance, and trust (25-30%)
- Describe Azure pricing, service level agreements and support (20-25%)

Taking, and successfully passing, Microsoft exam AZ-900 Azure Fundamentals awards the Microsoft Certified Azure Fundamentals badge, a foundation cloud computing qualification which does not expire!

Exam Objective 1 – Cloud Concepts

What is Cloud Computing?

So, what is cloud computing? Cloud computing is an Internet-driven delivery model for computing services. Cloud computing enables consumers to build or use systems and services operated by companies located around the world, at the click of a button. Microsoft's Azure is an example of a cloud computing platform.

Microsoft Azure, like other cloud platforms, provides core services such as:

- Storage for your files and databases, as well as the means to migrate them to the cloud. Disk space and the infrastructure to make it available for your use on demand.
- Compute Power – meaning the ability to build servers ready near-instantly for whatever you require. These servers are virtual – meaning multiple servers run on shared hardware in Microsoft's datacentres. A 'server' is not a single machine in cloud computing.
- Networking – Create secure connections between your cloud components to make everything work, as well as connections to the Internet for public connectivity to applications, and secure private connections from your office-based systems.

- Analytics – Cloud platforms gather performance and telemetry data, which you can analysis to improve your systems and services.

The list of services offered by Microsoft Azure is much larger than this, but the core service areas listed above are those you need to understand for Azure Fundamentals AZ-900.

Cloud Characteristics

Although the four areas listed above are the core of Cloud computing, certain characteristics are required to meet the definition of Cloud Computing.

Scalability

Scaling is the ability to near-instantly increase or reduce the capability of a system or service on-demand. This comes in two forms: Let us use the example of a virtual server, also known as a virtual machine or 'VM'. To 'Scale Up' is to increase the capability of an existing service – adding CPUs or memory to a virtual machine to meet an increase in demand for instance. 'Scale Down' would be the reverse of this, should demand reduce – these are also known as 'Vertical Scaling'.

'Scale Out' would be to build more virtual machines of the same type as the one already in existence, the meet the same increase in demand. 'Scaling In' would be the reverse of this, should demand reduce – this is known as 'Horizontal Scaling'.

Elasticity

Elasticity is the ability to scale dynamically in response to consumption – an elastic service should be able to increase resources as user demand increases and decrease them as that demand reduces. Elasticity is essentially automatic scaling.

Agility

There are two ways to provision resources in the Microsoft Azure Cloud – manually via the Azure Portal, or automatically via scripts or other programmatic requests such as API calls. Whichever you choose, there will be a time delay between the request for a resource, and that resource becoming available.

In the datacentre computing model, if you needed a new server you would order one from a manufacturer, await delivery, install and configure before eventually being able to use that server for its purpose. That process would have taken days or possibly weeks. With the agility of cloud computing, we can take advantage of Microsoft Azure and its underlying infrastructure to build servers and services in seconds or minutes.

Agility in the cloud means the ability to allocate or deallocate resources quickly, as you or your business requires.

Fault Tolerance

All cloud components whether they be web, virtual machines, databases, storage of any other of the myriad available, run on underlying infrastructure – physical servers, disks and networking housed in a purpose-built facility. Fault tolerance is the ability for a service running in the cloud to continue to run despite any component or service failures within the underlying infrastructure.

This may mean a virtual server moving automatically to a different underlying host system in the event of a component failure such as memory. It could also mean data being made available on a different physical disk in the event of errors or performance degradation on the disk upon which a service was previously running.

Using cloud services, you should not perceive any change as a result of failures that may occur with the underlying Microsoft Azure systems. Depending on the options you choose in configuration, this can even extend to your cloud services being tolerant of outages effecting whole datacentres, regions or geographic locations. Disruptions at greater scale are known as 'disaster', thus building a service to be disaster tolerant may be desirable, depending on your needs.

Disaster Recovery

Related to the above, disaster recovery is the ability to recover from issues significant enough they did cause an interruption in service. In simple terms, disaster recovery means having more than one application server, and more than one copy of your data. Then if one set of servers and data becomes unavailable, you can bring the second into service. With cloud computing you can automate the process to avoid service disruption by simply redirecting users.

You may also recover from disaster by recovering a service from Azure backups rather than maintaining standby services.

High Availability

High Availability means cloud services should be available for consumption for the overwhelming majority of the time. Downtime might include planned maintenance, patching, hardware and software upgrades, as well as unplanned system failures. Availability is a simple calculation of the amount of time a system was available as a percentage of the total time period overall. It is not unusual for Microsoft Azure services to offer 99.99% availability, meaning you should expect the service in question to be unavailable for less than 53 minutes per year.

I think we can agree, that would be 'High Availability'.

How Cloud Companies do it

If traditional datacentre-based tech costs a company so much more to run than cloud computing, how do Microsoft and the other providers do it cheaper? Economies of scale.

Microsoft operate Azure at the kind of scale where they can purchase the hardware they need for less than you or I, because they buy so much of it. They can negotiate rents on datacentre space for less than you or I, because they will sign longer-term leases. They have dedicated teams managing their hardware and software, instead of having third parties provide services to them as you or I might. Those prices per unit coming down thanks to Microsoft efficiencies benefit their customers enormously.

All that means Microsoft can offer, for example, a virtual machine running on shared hardware for a fraction of the cost you might pay to buy a server, host it somewhere, and maintain it appropriately. Customer savings can be maximised by only running what you need when you need it, so only paying when a service is in use.

CapEx vs OpEX

There are other advantages to operating your technology services following the cloud model. Assets you purchase are accounted for differently than services you consume. This comes down to the differences between Capital Expenditure (CapEx), and Operating Expenditure (OpEx).

CapEx

Capital Expenditure, or CapEx, is basically the purchase of assets you (or your company) then hold for their usable life. Such assets would include traditional datacentre hardware – servers, disk arrays, switches, firewalls, and everything else it takes to operate a modern datacentre. Typically,

CapEx costs associated with traditional datacentre deployments spike at the beginning with initial investment in hardware, and those initial costs are typically higher than the 'today' requirement as companies are likely to plan for growth over the life of the asset. So perhaps a server is over-specced by 30% to account to account for expected 5-year growth.

That approach means you pay for hardware capacity you do not use from day 1. All that spare capacity lies waiting, at least initially, but still generates a cost. That cost then decreases over time into the day to day running costs such as power and maintenance, which are OpEx costs.

OpEX

Operation Expenditure, or OpEx, is the expenditure associated with the running of a service – power and maintenance of systems being the example already offered for datacentre OpEx costs.

The OpEx model fits the cloud approach to infrastructure perfectly – all servers, disks and associated systems or services are rented on a pay as you go basis, with no initial investment upfront. Also, no need to buy more than you require, as the services scale to the demands of your users – no more wasted resources. The cloud service provider covers all operating costs within a single bill – power consumption and maintenance, for example.

Azure Pricing – Consumption Models

Azure pricing is based on a consumption model – pay only for what you use. No upront costs, as services do not incur a charge unless they are running, and the elastic nature of cloud computing means that any service you commission can scale from a zero start to supporting huge numbers of users as quickly as you need it to with no resource wasted or unnecessary costs.

Many services are priced as separate components for clarity. Virtual machines, for example, are priced based on type of system – amount of memory and CPU, plus an additional charge for attached storage. There may then be additional charges related to networking and other services attached to the machine. Listing all these separately gives the customer maximum flexibility and control, but also visibility when the bill comes through – it is easy to see at a glance where your money was spent in the cloud. All services are only charged for the amount of time they are used.

IaaS, PaaS & SaaS

Cloud services are typically badged 'as a Service', and you will see 'aaS' a good deal, and the Azure Fundamentals AZ-500 exam requires candidates be able to describe each as well as comparing the different service types with each other. Examples of high-level service types are:

Infrastructure as a Service (IaaS):

Think of IaaS as the rental of traditional infrastructure elements like servers, storage, networks, operating systems and such from a cloud service vendor. We can create virtual machines running Windows or Linux and install anything we need on them as required.

Using IaaS gives the customer freedom from hardware maintenance and hypervisor management, but everything beyond that is managed by the customer. The customer is in total control of systems running on managed infrastructure. Storage, networking, servers and the 21 irtualization technology are all infrastructure components, and all would be examples of IaaS. Azure VMs would be a specific example of IaaS.

Platform as a Service (PaaS):

The PaaS family of services provide on-demand environments for developing, testing, delivering, and managing software applications. The customer is responsible for applications and services, and the PaaS vendor provides the ability to deploy and run them.

PaaS lacks the total customer control of IaaS, but has the advantage of reducing customer responsibility to the application tier, with everything else managed by the cloud services vendor. The cloud service provider would manage the infrastructure components such as networking and virtualisation, as well as the platform components such as operating systems, middleware ad runtimes. Azure SQL would be an example of a PaaS service, a turnkey offering ready for customer data.

Software as a Service (SaaS):

SaaS covers the centrally hosted and managed software services provided direct to end-users. SaaS delivers software over the internet, on-demand, and typically on a subscription basis. Microsoft One Drive, Dropbox, WordPress, Office 365, and Amazon Kindle.

SaaS is used to minimize the operational cost to the maximum extent.

Cloud Deployment Models

There are three main flavours of Cloud Computing – Public, Private, and Hybrid. The Microsoft Azure Fundamentals AZ-900 exam requires that candidates understand the cloud deployment models, the differences between them, and the advantages and disadvantages of each.

Public Cloud

Public cloud services are owned and operated by a third-party cloud service provider. They deliver computing resources such as servers, software, and storage and as customers you never own any resources, pay as you go rental model with hardware shared with many customers. Public cloud provides a virtual datacentre over the internet. Microsoft Azure would be an example of a Public Cloud service.

The advantages of this model include zero capital expenditure (CapEx), high availability and agility, and all operational costs are bundled together – power, hardware maintenance, tech support for the platform and so forth.

Disadvantages may be found by those requiring higher levels of security or specific regulatory compliance – with shared infrastructure, some compromises are necessary, although cloud providers often have specific service offerings for those with more stringent requirements. The lack of ownership could also be seen as a disadvantage, depending on your point of view.

Private Cloud

Private Cloud services are those built to be exclusively used inside a single business or organisation. A private cloud may be physically located in company-operated premises or hosted by a third-party. Private Clouds typically consist of server and storage infrastructure, upon which many servers and services are virtualised. To truly be considered a private cloud rather than merely a traditional datacentre deployment, the philosophy of cloud around availability, elasticity and on-demand deployment should be adopted.

The advantages of private cloud are all around control. The private cloud can be designed and built precisely to meet the requirements of its consumer, no compromises. Any business scenario ca be catered for and any security or compliance requirement met precisely.

Disadvantages are predictably around cost – the initial investment for a private cloud deployment will be significant and will be a CapEx cost. A reliance on inite infrastructure also brings with it a reduction in operational agility – you need more processing power? You are either going to have to buy too much in the first place and pay the cost, or suffer delays while more compute resource is ordered, delivered, and configured. With everything being provided 'in-house', there will be a more significant support cost to bear as well as a need for highly skilled staff.

Hybrid Cloud

Hybrid cloud is a combination of public and private clouds, bridged together by technology that allows data and applications to be shared between them. Hybrid cloud provides flexibility and more deployment options to the business and could represent the best of both previous options.

Advantages of the hybrid approach include the flexibility to host services in their best location – any service with specific requirements around technology, security or compliance can be hosted in private cloud for maximum control, and any service with standard requirements can be hosted in public cloud to reduce costs.

Existing infrastructure could also be repurposed for cost efficiency.

Disadvantages again come down to cost, the need for highly skilled staff, and likely the most complex configuration of the three.

Exam Objective 2 – Azure Core Services

In this section we will learn about the Azure core services, satisfying objective two of the exam requirements, to be able to describe Azure core services. This subject area is worth around a third of the available marks in the exam and forms the foundation of the Azure service offering. It is definitely worth taking your time here to make sure the material has sunk in before moving on.

Geographies, Regions & Availability Zones

Fundamentally the language of location, our guide to Azure concepts begins with the geographical. By the end of this opening section, you will be able to:

- Describe the Datacentre
- Describe Regions and Region Pairs
- Describe Geographies
- Describe Availability Zones
- Describe the usage of the core components
- Describe the benefits of the core components

The Data Centre

The Data Centre in Azure terms is really no different to the traditional data centre. When you build Azure services, be they SQL databases, Web services, virtual machines or storage, those services run on physical servers in Microsoft's physical data centres – purpose-built facilities hosting massive amounts of technology infrastructure. Typical data centres hold massive quantities of servers and storage, and provide power, cooling and networking infrastructure to support those systems.

The data centre is the basic building block of the Microsoft Azure global service.

Regions

A number of data centres in relatively close proximity, connected to each other via high-throughput links, is collectively known as a Region. Microsoft have many regions of various sizes, distributed across the world. Some regions can consist of a single data centre, but most include many separate facilities. There are more than fifty Azure Regions spread across the globe, with more being added all the time.

Region selection is typically a decision made based on user proximity – less network latency between user and server results in better performance. Location is a ley consideration, as well as a mandatory decision point when commissioning new services. Azure's speed test service can assist in establishing the best performing data centre for your location.

Some services are not available in all regions, in which case it would be sensible to select the best fit available for your use case, positioning the service as close as possible to its consumers. There are also services, such as Azure Active Directory (AAD) and Traffic Manager for DNS routing, which are global services, and as such are not assigned to a specific region. Azure again provides tools to establish which services are available in which regions, to aid the user in making the best selection for their purposes.

Specialist secure services for Government are provided via Government Regions, such as US DoD Central and US Gov Virginia for example, and Partner Regions are made available for the more stringent requirements of Chinese consumers, or those seeking to do cloud business in China. Additional qualifying criteria are required for access to these services.

Availability Zones

Availability zones are a feature of Azure Regions that group physically separate facilities. For example, an Azure Region might have 3 sets of data centre facilities which are physically removed enough from each other to offer service resilience. Let us for the sake of the example say there are four distinct facilities in a Region, all are 100 miles apart from each other. Each would be defined as an availability zone.

Perhaps within a Region a single data centre could be flooded, experience a power outage or some other unforeseen disaster, but the others would continue uninterrupted. Spreading your Azure resources across availability zones makes them resistant to Azure service interruptions within a region.

So, for high-availability deployments, it is possible to build a VM within a Region in Availability Zone #1, then build a second in Availability Zone #2. Doing so would maintain the advantages of high throughput links between data centres within a region but provide resilience against data centre failure. Without the availability zone decision being taken, it is possible all virtual machines could be deployed within the same data centre, or even on the same underlying physical host server, greatly increasing the exposure of any Azure service built to the risk of physical failure.

Some Azure services, like Azure SQL and storage are zonally redundant 'out of the box' – during setup of SQL or storage, simply checking an option for zone redundancy will see all data replicated to a secondary zone. IN the event of a data centre level failure, service consumers would not be aware.

Not all Regions support availability zones, as at least three zones within an Azure Region are required, with a zone being one or more data centre facilities in relatively close proximity.

Region Pairs

Each Azure Region has a Region Pair, with paired regions being at least 300 miles apart from each other to mitigate against larger scale geographical disaster events such as earthquakes. Microsoft configure the Region Pairs, with each pair residing within the same geographical region, with the exception of Brazil South which is paired with the US.

Similar to Availability Zone replication previously, some Azure services are capable of platform-provided replication across Region Pairs with a simple click of a checkbox during setup to mitigate against Region level failures.

Another advantage of Region Pairs is Microsoft scheduling updates to their services across Region pairs, ensuring that only one partner is subjected to any scheduled update at any one time, which mitigates against the unforeseen consequences of an update gone bad. Once any update has been proven successful, the partner Region can also be updated.

Replication of services and data across Region Pairs is recommended. Replication across any two regions is possible, but replication across a region pair offers the additional advantages around latency and update scheduling. It is theoretically possible that A deployment to a US region and a European Region could see Azure updates made to both simultaneously, resulting in possible service disruption. This can be avoided with a Region Pair.

Examples of Region Pairs include:

East US	-	West US
UK West	-	UK South
North Europe (IRL)	-	West Europe (NL)
East Asia	-	Southeast Asia

Region Pairs are not always located within a country but must be close enough to maintain high speed connectivity, whilst distant enough to ensure isolation from natural disasters.

Geographies

Microsoft Azure Geographies are groupings of Regions and Region Pairs. Each Azure Geography represents a discrete Azure market, typically containing two or more regions.

Azure Geographies ensure data residency for those requiring it, sovereignty, resilience, and a consistent foundation for any compliance requirements Azure customers may need to satisfy. Being made up of multiple Regions, they are also fault tolerant to Region-wide failures.

Geographies are global areas such as:

- Americas
- Europe
- Asia Pacific
- Middle East and Africa

Each Region belongs to a single Geography.

Azure Resources

In this section we will satisfy the exam objectives related to your understanding of Azure resources. By the end of this section, you will be able to:

- Describe Azure Resources
- Describe Azure Resource Groups
- Describe Azure Resource Manager
- Describe the benefits of using Azure resources, resource groups and resource manager.

These are some of the first building blocks of Microsoft Azure that you will encounter when commissioning services in the cloud.

When you consume services in Azure, whether they be SQL databases, Web applications, virtual machines or any other service, the cloud products, components, and services you are using can be expressed as resources.

Resources are objects used to manage services in Microsoft Azure, and represent a service lifecycle – they can be created, updated, and managed, and ultimately deleted when no longer required. Configuration settings you make against your Azure services would be saved as properties of the underlying Azure resource.

Resources in Azure can also be represented by JSON templates (JavaScript Object Notation), a simple file comprised of properties and values.

There are four common properties for Azure Resources in JSON templates:

- TYPE
- APIVERSION
- NAME
- LOCATION

A mandatory property of any Azure resource is a resource group.

Resource Groups

A Resource Group is a parent container in which resources reside. A management construct used to simplify billing and provide a logical means of grouping together related Azure components for your convenience, irrespective of their technology or location.

Resources are typically grouped by:

- Type: Less common, since whilst all SQL databases (for example) might have similar technology requirements, they are unlikely to all have the same access requirements.
- Lifecycle: App Environment resource grouping for development and production, for example, allows separate management of the resources in a group by their environment – policies, scripts, access management and so forth.

- Department: Resources are sometimes grouped together based on the owner within your organisation.
- Billing: Resources are often grouped based on the business unit paying the bill for the resources. A separate group could be created for each cost centre.

The decision is driven by each organisation and is best decided based on your specific requirements.

Personal recommendation – group by technology. All elements related to core infrastructure should be grouped as 'Core'. With service specific components grouped together for easier management. All other considerations can be captured using tags, which we will cover later in this book!

Access control can be managed at a Resource group level, using the Azure portal or command line interface (CLI) tools to grant access to users to all resources within a group from the group level.

Each Azure resource must be in a resource group but can only be a member of one resource group at a time. Resource groups also have a location assigned, but the location of the group itself is only used to store metadata, it has no bearing on or relationship with the resources within that group. Resources in a resource group can reside in different locations, there is no need to maintain a commonality of location within a resource group.

Resources can be moved freely between groups, so any decision made can be easily revisited. It is not possible to nest resource groups, and resource grouping strategy should be based on organizational need. Most organisations choose a combination of the approaches discussed previously, with an amalgamation of service and environment being popular.

Azure Resource Manager

Azure resources can be built using a number of technologies:

- The Azure Portal
- REST APIs
- PowerShell
- The Command Line Interface (CLI)
- SDKs

All these tools interact with the Azure Resource Manager (ARM) to commission the products and services requested – sending the underlying JSON template to the resource manager to create the service(s). The Azure Resource Manager also checks Azure Active Directory to ensure you have sufficient privileges to request the operation being requested.

Azure Resource Manager is an internal service responsible for building and managing Azure resources.

Azure Compute Services

This section covers the AZ-900 exam requirements related to Azure compute services, which include the ability to describe available Azure compute products, including:

- Virtual Machines
- Virtual Machine Scale Sets
- Container Instances
- Kubernetes
- App Services
- Functions

Azure Compute is a category of on-demand services used to deploy cloud-based applications and services, as well as infrastructure as a service (IaaS) offerings that mimic traditional data centre server deployments.

Virtualisation

To understand Azure virtual machines, we need an appreciation of virtualization as a technology.

In the traditional server model, you buy a server and install it in your data centre. You then install an operating system and whatever apps and services are required to make it functional. That server is now ready for its purpose, but is typically ring-fenced for that purpose. It is likely to be operating far beyond its potential, and not to be heavily utilized. On the flip side, were you to try to run multiple apps and services from that single server, you would likely suffer from resource contention – the various services needing access to server resources at the same time, negatively impacting performance.

Virtualisation removes the 1:1 relationship between an operating system and the underlying server hardware. In the virtualization model, virtualization software is installed on the native server operating system, which then permits the creation of multiple virtual machines within it. That means you can run multiple servers on a single physical system, with each being unaware of the others. Each can be given access to specific quantities of physical resources to maintain performance of all as necessary.

Virtualisation brings cost advantages in running multiple servers on each physical system and allows better use of resources since every physical server can be driven closer to its capacity. It also makes it possible to run different operating systems on a single physical server – both Windows and Linux, for example.

Azure Virtual Machines

Virtualisation on Microsoft Azure takes the form of Azure Virtual Machines. Microsoft make various machine images available to Azure users, as well as other Azure customers making them available on the Azure marketplace. It is also possible to build your own machine images to specific organizational requirements, which can then be reused to build multiple virtual machines.

Azure Virtual Machines are considered IaaS, meaning you retain responsibility for the operation of the server, and all software upon it – from the operating system through to any applications you have installed. This provides total control of the system. Azure Virtual Machines are best used for custom deployments requiring bespoke system configurations, and 'life and shift' migration scenarios to transition to Azure.

More or less any scenario you can imagine can be accommodated by an Azure Virtual Machine. Any application you can install on an operating system using a physical server can be accomplished on a virtual machine, be it a web application or service, a desktop application, a database or... well... anything else!

Virtual Machines score highly for customer control and configuration freedom, but have their drawbacks too. Most notably in terms of scalability – one machine is one machine, and whilst it is possible to scale up by adding memory, CPU, and disk, it is not so easy to scale out.

Which is why Microsoft Azure brought us Virtual Machine Scale Sets.

Azure Virtual Machine Scale Sets

Virtual Machine Scale Sets provide a service where an Azure VM image is installed on multiple Azure Virtual Machines, which are positioned behind a load-balancer. A load-balancer, as you can probably guess from the name, is a virtual network device that takes incoming network connections from users or applications and distributes them across the available systems in the scale set. So, in this scenario you would achieve higher availability by creating multiple servers in a scale set, functioning as one.

Static scale sets can be created by specifying a number of virtual machines in a scale set, which remains constant regardless of application load, or by using autoscaling to allow the number of virtual machines to increase and/or decrease based on demand.

Virtual Machine Scale Sets are also an IaaS Azure offering and are ideal for scaling out Virtual Machine based services such as web services, batch processing and anything else that needs to respond to peaks and troughs in user-demand.

Containers

Containers are another Azure Compute service offering, different from Virtual Machines in several key respects.

Containerisation services run on physical servers, much like virtualization software, but instead of running multiple virtual machines on a single physical server, it is possible to install a containerization runtime and subsequently run multiple containers on a single physical server. Each container is a self-contained unit capable of running an application. As a service consumer you are only responsible for the application with all other services, such as network connectivity and the underlying host operating system, managed by Microsoft and invisible to you.

Where Virtual machines emulate the underlying hardware of a physical server, containers emulate the host operating system. This makes containers lighter weight than virtual machines, which brings a reduction in development effort, zero maintenance outside of the application, and much-reduced storage and compute requirements.

Azure Container Instances

Azure Container Instances allow the user to take an application and any configuration required to make it run in the manner your organization requires, and create an image suitable for deployment to a container repository. A container repository is simple storage for containerised applications.

Much like Virtual Machines, the Azure marketplace makes customer images for many popular applications available to anyone in just a few clicks.

Once you have your containerized application, it can be pushed to an Azure Container Instance, which will build a container group automatically – a Virtual Machine under the hood to host your container applications. Those containers can then be made available to users as required.

Azure Container Services is the easiest and fastest way to run containerized applications in Microsoft Azure. It is also the first PaaS service we have come across, with all underlying infrastructure components managed by Microsoft. Container Instances are sometimes referred to as 'serverless' – although there are servers involved, they are not servers you need to manage when deploying containers to instances.

Azure Container Instances are ideal for small and simple web applications, background processing jobs and scripts.

Container instances offer less control and configurability than either Virtual Machines or Scale Sets and are not capable of autoscaling, with a maximum of twenty nodes in a scale set. The serverless aspect makes them extremely attractive for small or simple applications, as well as the detachment from the operating system and hardware being very helpful for portability.

Kubernetes

Kubernetes is another container deployment solution, similar to Container Instances in many respects. Kubernetes can take your containerized application image and deploy it across multiple nodes (Virtual Machines) automatically, exposing the resulting cluster of nodes to users via a load-balancer.

As with Scale Sets, both static and autoscaling options are available, depending on your requirements.

Kubernetes is an open-source container orchestration platform, developed initially by Google and available on all cloud platforms. Considered a PaaS cloud service offering, it is highly scalable and customizable, designed for deploying container apps at scale.

Kubernetes represents a highly sophisticated Azure compute option – almost as configurable as a Virtual Machine, with autoscaling available and capable of far greater scale than Container Instances. As a more complex technology, Kubernetes requires a skilled team to maintain it.

App Service

The Azure App Service has a much lower maintenance requirement than the compute options that have gone before, and its main use case is Web services and Web applications. Simply package your app, and deploy to App Service. App Service will then present the resulting application nodes to users.

App Service is designed to provide enterprise-class Web application services and, like Kubernetes, is considered a PaaS offering. App Service supports multiple programming languages and containers, making it suitable for a broad range of applications and technologies, as well as making it accessible to developers without a need for a specific skillset. Spinning up a new app service is a matter of accessing the Azure Portal, creating a new Awe App, providing a name, a runtime, a location and specifying the size of Virtual Machine you want to power the app, and away you go.

Azure App Service being light on configuration is convenient for getting off the ground, but also means a lack of access to the underlying infrastructure and a lack of configurability, which could be a disadvantage to some. It is capable of auto-scaling, and is both a powerful and accessible compute technology suitable for any deployment where a lack of visibility of the underlying infrastructure stack is not a concern.

Azure Functions

Also known as Function Apps, Azure Functions are similar to App Service, but execute small pieces of code as apps – package your code and deploy as a Function App. The Function App will then be published to nodes and made available for services to call.

Azure Functions are considered PaaS, but are also serverless, as they are configured and operate in such a way that the underlying infrastructure is not exposed to developers or consuming services. If there are no calls being made to the Function Apps, no network connectivity means no network utilization, which means no charges.

Azure Functions have two pricing options:

- Consumption-based – traditional Azure pay-per-use model where each call invokes a charge, or;
- Dedicated plan via App Service – a flat fee irrespective of level of consumption.

The more cost-effective option for you will be based on your use case.

Azure Functions are designed for micro or nano-service deployments, and their serverless nature makes them easy to maintain – set and forget, as we sometimes say. Autoscaling for performance and availability is an option, and the scaling capabilities of Azure Functions are greater than those of either Kubernetes or App Service.

Azure Compute Summary

Azure offers multiple compute options, suitable for any use-case.

Virtual Machines are IaaS, and give total control to the user. Custom software, any requirement, any size for any purpose. Build it yourself and run whatever service you see fit with total freedom and control, at the cost of a greater maintenance overhead and a need for specialized skills to execute. VM Scale Sets are also IaaS, and an extension of the above, used for auto-scaling Virtual Machines, for either performance, availability, or resilience.

Container Instances are PaaS, ad offer simple container hosting. Easy to spin up, but lacking in scale options. The containerization aspect removes the configuration freedom of a Virtual Machine, but also the need for infrastructure skills to deploy apps using them.

Kubernetes is also PaaS, and is a more scalable container orchestration option than Container Instances, sharing the same lack of configuration freedom, but freedom from infrastructure management.

App Service is PaaS, and designed for hosting simple containerized Web apps, with a variety of runtimes available. Easy to spin up, and quick to deploy.

Azure Functions are ideal for running small pieces of code as applications, and their serverless nature means costs can be minimized with the consumption-based charging model.

If the right Azure compute service for you is not already evident from your use-case, Microsoft provide some excellent flow charts and decision trees to help you arrive at the best-fit technology for your needs.

Azure Networking

This section covers the AZ-900 exam requirements related to Azure networking services, which include the ability to describe available Azure networking products, including:

- Virtual Network (VNet)
- Load Balancers
- VPN Gateways
- Application Gateways
- Content Delivery Networks

Azure networking is a service category that provides the capability to connect cloud and on-prem resources, protect and monitor services and facilitate application delivery.

Azure Virtual Networks

Azure Virtual Networks (or VNets) are a cloud representation of a physical network, in the same way as a Virtual Machine is a cloud representation of a physical server. Azure Virtual Networks provide the means to connect, protect and monitor Azure resources, enabling access both from other Azure components and the outside world.

Azure Virtual Networks can be segmented into separate subnets, and that segmentation can be an advantage for many reasons:

- Management of IP address allocation.
- Grouping of resources based on access requirements – providing isolation, segmentation, communication, filtering and routing.
- Subnets also represent a security boundary, adding a layer at which network security configuration can be applied.

Subnets can be secured using Network Security Groups (NSGs) or Application Security Groups (ASGs). Both of these are discussed later in this book.

There are also many reasons for creating multiple VNets, most notably that a VNet can only exist in a single region and can only contain resources from the same region. Running applications and services in multiple regions will instantly drive a requirement for multiple VNets.

Connecting VNets to each other can be achieved by using VNet Peering, or VPN Gateways – there are positives and negatives to both approaches, but for the purposes of Azure Fundamentals you need only understand that there are two options for establishing connectivity between VNets!

VPN Gateway

Also known as a Virtual Network Gateway, a VPN Gateway is the means by which you can securely connect your on-prem datacentre or business premises to your Azure Virtual Network. This communication takes place over the public Internet, but is entirely encrypted.

VPN Gateways can also be used to connect Azure Virtual Networks, though this approach is less common than VNet Peering.

Azure Load Balancer

As the name suggests, an Azure Load Balancer balances load or, perhaps more helpfully, distributes network traffic across multiple destination systems or services as you require. For example, if you have two Virtual Machines configured to serve a web site, you can configure an Azure Load Balancer to ensure that all traffic coming from the public Internet is evenly distributed to both. An Azure Load Balancer is not limited to Virtual Machines as destination services though, traffic can also be routed to applications and other services.

The advantages of load balancing fall broadly into two categories – performance and availability. Using a load balancer makes it easy to add additional virtual machines to a configuration, and the load balancer can be updated to distribute traffic between the increased number of Virtual Machines. Health checks can be used to establish the availability of a Virtual Machine and, in the event of a failure, no traffic would be sent to the failed Virtual Machine.

Azure Load Balancers support both TCP and UDP traffic, as well as both Internal and External connections.

Application Gateway

An Azure Application Gateway is very similar to Azure Load Balancer, in so far as it also distributes network traffic across multiple destination systems or services as per its configuration. An Azure Application Gateway is designed and optimized for Web traffic – HTTTP and HTTPS.

Application Gateways are application aware, and offer additional features over and above Azure Load Balancers, including:

- Web Application Firewall (WAF)
- Redirection services
- Session affinity - user 1 is directed to Server1 and is then always serviced by Server1 for the duration of the session. Also known as 'Sticky Sessions'
- URL Routing – yourwebsite.com/pages can be configured to be served by one server, with yourwebsite.com/account served by another
- SSL termination – SSL can be terminated at the gateway, removing the overhead

of decrypting the traffic from the destination system

These features are all useful and interesting, but not required for the Azure Fundamentals exam. Just remember that Application Gateway is a load balancer designed and optimized for web application traffic.

Content Delivery Networks

A Content Delivery Network, or CDN, is a networking service used to improve performance of web applications.

In a traditional model, a web service, website, or application is comprised of static and dynamic content, hosted on a server in a specific location. In this model, users will connect to the server with each request, and download all the data required – images and HTML in the case of a simple website. Each request takes time to be served, and generates load on the webserver. User experience is inconsistent owing to network latency, so a user who is geographically closer to the server is likely to see much better response times than a user who is far away.

Enter CDN! A globally distributed Microsoft Azure service, where static and/or frequently accessed material can be stored for faster access owing to reduced latency. Microsoft have well over one hundred CDN locations, referred to as Points of Presence (or 'POP'). Users will connect to your website, but any content available at their local POP location will be served from there, improving response times for the user as well as reducing the load on your web server.

Azure Networking Summary

Azure Virtual Networks (VNets) emulate physical networks in the cloud, providing grouping, filtering and segmentation of network resources via subnets.

Azure VPN Gateway is a means of securely connecting on-prem locations with Azure Virtual Networks], as well as each other. VNet Peering also available for inter-VNet connectivity.

Azure Load Balancers distribute traffic across multiple destination servers or services, and are designed for non-HTTP(S) scenarios.

Azure Application Gateways distribute traffic across multiple destination servers or services and are HTTP (Web) optimised with additional service options available.

Azure Content Delivery Network (CDN) is a global content caching and distribution network, used to store web application content closer to the user for reduced latency and improved user experience.

Azure Storage

There are many Azure services designed for the storage of structured, semi-structured and unstructured data. The Azure Fundamentals exam requires that you possess the skills to:

Describe the benefits, and use of:

- Blob storage, including storage tiers
- File storage
- Table storage
- Queue storage
- Disk storage

Each storage type is designed with a particular data type in mind.

Structured data is that which has a formal and consistent structure, with relationships between datasets that are well enough defined that they could be represented in a diagram. This is the sort of data you would expect to find in a database.

Semi-structured data may be less relational than structured data but will still have some commonality – perhaps a specific index or ID column.

Unstructured data is your mixed-bag folder with images, movies, executables, and files from your preferred productivity applications.

If you do not know what type of data you have, there is a very good chance it is unstructured.

Microsoft have a storage solution especially designed for that!

Azure Blob Storage

Azure Blob storage is optimized for storing large quantities of unstructured data, such as images, text, movies, or other binary data. The term 'Blob' stands for **B**inary **L**arge **Ob**ject and covers more or less any classification of data outside of a database.

In Azure, Blob storage is subdivided into containers – which are nothing more than boxes to put your data in. Analogous to S3 buckets in AWS, or folders in a traditional file system. Azure Blob has three storage tiers:

- Hot – used to store frequently accessed data
- Cool – used to store infrequently accessed data, this tier has lower availability but higher durability than 'hot'
- Archive – the lowest cost tier, used to store rarely accessed data, or data which may never be accessed by has to be retained.

Blob Storage is accessed by applications and users using HTTP requests.

Azure Queue Storage

Azure Queue Storage allows applications to send individual messages to a queue to be picked up and processed by other applications or services at their own pace, and asynchronously. This approach can reduce load on the originating application and underlying infrastructure, as well as enabling a compartmentalization of the end-to-end process, and the potential to hand off the background processing to an application or service better suited to completing it.

Azure Queue Storage is designed for small datasets to be stored temporarily as messages, and scalable asynchronous processing. A simple service, with a specific use case.

Azure Table Storage

Azure Table Storage was designed for semi-structured data, enabling users and applications to output data into tables. Unlike a relational database, there are no joins and no schema, just semi-structured data arranged into tables. These database types are also known as NoSQL databases.

You can work, insert, update, and operate the data in a semi-structured form without the need for foreign joins, keys, relationships, or strict schemas.

Azure Table Storage is designed for fast access, and even very large datasets can be accessed very efficiently using compound keys to reference rows. Very scalable for such a simple service.

Microsoft provide a large number of programming interfaces and SDKs to interact with Azure Table Storage, making it very easy to access programmatically when developing Azure solutions.

Azure File Storage

Also known simply as Azure Files, Azure File Storage is essentially your traditional CIFS / SMB file system in the cloud. A hierarchical folder and file structure for unstructured data, which should be familiar to any computer user.

Azure Files works similarly to Blob Storage, except that applications and users connect to shares using SMB, rather than containers using HTTP. Once there, files are accessed from the shares. Mapping drives to UNC paths from consuming systems simplifies connectivity and access.

There are two main scenarios that suit Azure Files:

- Extension of on-prem file shares to the cloud
- List and Shift of application data without the need to update the application to

use Blob storage instead of traditional file systems.

And that summarises the drivers for the Blob vs. Azure Files decision point – use Blob storage unless you need connectivity to a traditional file share via SMB.

Azure Storage Account

The Azure Storage Account is the foundation into which storage services are deployed. The Azure Storage Account covers a group of services, including the four we have just covered:

- Azure Blob
- Azure Queue
- Azure Table
- Azure Files

Storage can be used for files, messages, and semi-structured data, and is highly scalable to petabytes of data. It is also highly durable – if selecting locally redundant storage (LRS), 99.999999999% uptime is guaranteed. That is 11 nines, with up to sixteen available with the right options selected. Making a loss of data next to impossible. It is also the cheapest cost per GB available.

Azure Disk Storage

Azure Disk Storage is used by Virtual Machines. A Windows VM, for example, may have drives C:, D:, E: and G: - those virtual disks will be stored on one or more physical disks, and that service in Azure is called Azure Disk Storage. Basically disk emulation in the cloud, offering persistent storage for Virtual Machines that survives a reboot.

Azure Disk Storage offers different disk sizes and types, such as SSD and HDD, as well as a number of performance tiers which vary in cost. Non-critical systems and development environments can use lower tier Azure Disk Storage to reduce cost.

Disks can also be managed or unmanaged. Unmanaged disks are stored at a file level in Azure Blob Storage, and are classified as unmanaged as they are not managed by a cloud service provider, they must be managed by the customer themselves. Managed disks tend to be the more popular option here, with Microsoft managing all the backend Blobs and files supporting Azure Disk Storage, for a modest fee.

Azure Storage Services – Summary

An Azure Storage Account is highly scalable and durable and is built from a group of sub-services in Bob, Files, Queue and Table Storage.

Azure Blob is good general-purpose storage for most scenarios, accessed via HTTP.

Azure Files provides file shares in the cloud, accessed via SMB. This is a good fit for legacy connectivity requirements.

Azure Queue is a service used for storing small datasets as messages for asynchronous processing.

Azure Table is a scalable NoSQL storage solution for semi-structured data.

Azure Disk is a disk emulation service for Virtual Machines in the cloud.

Azure Database Services

In this section we will learn about the database services available in Microsoft Azure, satisfying the exam objectives to be able to describe the benefits and usage of:

- Azure Cosmos DB
- Azure SQL Databases
- Azure Databases for MySQL
- Azure Databases for PostgreSQL
- Azure SQL Managed Instance

In the previous section we learned about the three different types of data – unstructured, semi-structured and structured. When it comes to database services, we are only dealing with semi-structured or structured data.

Structured data is that which has a formal and consistent structure, with relationships between datasets that are well enough defined that they could be represented in a diagram. This is the sort of data you would expect to find in a relational database.

Semi-structured data may be less relational than structured data but will still have some commonality – perhaps a specific index or ID column. This kind of data is found in NoSQL databases.

Microsoft Azure has database services suitable for both.

Azure Cosmos DB

Cosmos DB is a NoSQL solution for semi-structured data, similar to Azure Table Storage but that data is stored and access by users and applications from collections in Cosmos DB, rather than tables in Azure Table Storage.

The primary feature of Cosmos DB over Azure Table Storage is its geographical replication. Cosmos DB is available in many regions. With a check of a box, data can be replicated to other Azure regions for availability, performance, or resilience. Global read/writes are possible, with clients connecting to the closest replica. This also makes Cosmos DB ultra-low latency – sub

10ms, making it a great choice for real-time applications.

Cosmos DB is globally distributed, schema-less NoSQL, with broad API availability including SQL, MongoDB, Cassandra, Gremlin and Table Storage. It is designed for highly responsive and real-time application deployments with low latency requirements, as well as multi-region apps.

Azure SQL Database

Used for storing structured data in Azure. Data is stored in SQL in tables, with each table entity having a defined schema. Once tables are defined, relationships between those tables can also be established. A Cloud version of SQL based on the most recent stable release of SQL, albeit less feature-rich than the full version of SQL server you could build yourself.

Azure SQL Database is a PaaS offering with rich query capabilities as well as high performance and reliability. It is a fully managed and secure SQL offering, allowing you to focus on building applications and services which require relational databases, rather than managing the infrastructure supporting those relational databases.

Backups and monitoring are easily achieved with minimal overhead.

Tools familiar to on-prem SQL users still exist in Azure but have been re-imagined. SQL Reporting Services becomes Power BI, Integration Services becomes Data Factory and Analysis Services... well... that's still Analysis Services!

Azure SQL

Azure SQL is a family of relational database services, of which the Azure SQL Database service we just learned about is one. Azure SQL Database offers a subset of features provided by the latest release of Microsoft SQL – if you find that a feature you need is not available in Azure SQL Database, you might elect to consume an Azure SQL Managed Instance.

Azure SQL Managed Instance is a fully Microsoft Managed SQL instance, with all the features of on-prem SQL server and Microsoft doing all the configuration work for you. The service comes at a premium, but if you need fully featured SQL this is likely to be a good option for you.

Azure also offers a SQL Data Warehouse service option, used for Big Data – vast quantities of data and the execution of complex queries against it. More on that in the Big Data section later.

It is possible to run SQL on a VM as an IaaS on Azure and doing so comes with many of the advantages of the other cloud SQL services – for example, backup, replication and monitoring at the click of a button.

There are also options for migrating existing databases to the cloud, including DB for MySQL and DB for PostgreSQL.

Azure Database Services Summary

Microsoft Azure offers many database services, geared toward specific customer performance and technology requirements.

Azure Cosmos DB is a globally distributed NoSQL database solution with ultra-low latency. Perfect for real time applications, and serverless!

Azure SQL Database is a reliable relational database offering based on the most recent release of Microsoft SQL, but with a somewhat reduced feature set.

Azure Database for MySQL is a version of Azure SQL optimised for the MySQL database engine, making it perfect for MySQL migrations to Azure.

Azure Database for PostgreSQL is a version of Azure SQL optimised for the PostgreSQL database engine, making it perfect for PostgreSQL migrations to Azure.

Azure SQL Managed Instances are fully featured SQL Server deployments to Azure, completely Microsoft managed PaaS. If you see an exam question on Azure SQL, Azure SQL Managed Instance is highly likely to be the answer – Microsoft love this service!

It is also possible to run SQL on an Azure VM, IaaS-style, but with the cloud advantages of monitoring, backup, and replication minus the usual complexities.

Finally, SQL Data Warehouse – a Massively Parallel Processing (MPP) version of SQL server designed for Big Data – huge volumes of data and complex queries.

The Azure Marketplace

A short section, but the AZ-900 Azure Fundamentals exam requires that you be able to describe the Azure Marketplace, as well as usage scenarios.

The Azure Marketplace is an online catalogue of services, full solutions, and templates for specific technologies available for purchase by Azure customers. Built by Microsoft as well as third-party vendors, you could even template your Azure solution and make it available to other Azure customers via the Marketplace!

Products are available at the click of a button, from simple to complex. IaaS, PaaS, and SaaS products are available – it is highly likely you will find a template to help you on the road to your Azure developed service. Any software licenses required by products purchased from the Marketplace will be included in the advertised cost, and Microsoft will see to the appropriate licensing of Marketplace products automatically.

Azure IoT

The Internet of Things (IoT) is a network of Internet-connected devices embedded in everyday object, which enables the sending and receiving of data – usually settings and telemetry.

Does your fridge tell you when you are out of milk? Maybe your lights or heating switch on according to a schedule, or your car can be locked by an app on your smartphone – that will be the Internet of Things in action.

Azure Fundamentals requires that you be able to describe the benefits and usage scenarios of Azure IoT services, including:

- IoT Hub
- IoT Central
- Azure Sphere

Azure IoT Hub

Azure IoT Hub allows for bi-directional communication between the Azure Cloud, and IoT devices, which empowers solution developers to parse that data for analysis, insights, monitoring and the development of custom applications and solutions in the IoT space.

There are several aspects of Azure IoT Hub that you should remember for the Azure Fundamentals exam:

- IoT Hub is a managed Azure service for bi-directional IoT communications
- IoT Hub is a PaaS Azure offering
- It is highly secure, stable and reliable
- It integrates with a huge number of Azure services

- IoT Hub includes SDKs for many popular languages, including C, C#, Java, Python and Node.js
- IoT Hub supports several protocols, including HTTPS, AMQP and MQTT

Axure IoT Central

IoT Central offers the same capabilities as IoT Hub for gathering data from IoT devices, the difference is that IoT Central has been designed for those who do not wish to develop their own IoT applications from scratch.

IoT Central holds templates for applications, and is an application delivery platform for IoT, for device management and centralisation.

The IoT Central App platform is a SaaS Azure service, with many industry-specific application templates available and no need for skilled staff or in-depth technical knowledge. It is used for connecting, managing, and monitoring IoT devices and is highly secure, scalable, and reliable.

Azure IoT Central is built on top of IoT Hub, as well as dozens of other Azure services under the hood.

Azure Sphere

Azure Sphere is a set of components that facilitate the build of IoT applications. Microsoft provides specifications to manufacturers to include in chipsets of their products. The resulting Azure Sphere-certified chips include built-in Microsoft security, and the Azure Sphere OS that runs on top adds layers of protection as well as security updates. Your IoT application would then run on top of the Azure Sphere OS.

The Azure Sphere security service brokers trust for IoT communications, detects threats, and maintains device security. It also enables your administrators and developers to securely update IoT devices using the security service.

Azure Sphere enables secure end to end IoT solutions from the device chipset, through the Linux-based Azure Sphere OS, providing trusted device to cloud communications.

Azure IoT Services Summary

For the Azure Fundamentals exam, only an appreciation of what the available services are, and in what circumstances you would use them, is required.

IoT Hub is a PaaS managed Azure service for bi-directional communications with IoT devices.

IoT Central is a SaaS IoT application platform with many templates, used when you do not want to develop your own IoT applications.

Azure Sphere is an end-to-end IoT management solution, from chipset to secure communications.

Azure Big Data and Analytics

There are three key Azure services designed for the processing of Big Data. The Azure Fundamentals exam requires that you possess the skills to:

Describe the benefits, and use of:

- Azure Synapse Analytics
- Azure HDInsight
- Azure Databricks

Let us start with an overview of Big Data. Big Data is a group of technologies that enable the extraction, processing and analysis of datasets that are too large to be managed by traditional software products.

There are three key aspects of datasets requiring a Big Data approach, and the closer to the right of each category we get, the better a fit the Big Data approach will be:

- Volume: Are we talking MB, GB, TB or PB?
- Variety: How structured is your data? Is it in Tables or Databases, or unstructured like images and audio, or video and social media feeds?
- Velocity: Is your data batch processed, periodic, near real-time or in real-time?

Ending up in the right of any category will make traditional software and approaches to analytics likely a poor fit.

Data engineers will start their process by establishing data locations – identifying databases, services and files which contribute to their source dataset. From there, data will be ingested, transformed into a coherent information set and stored appropriately before being made available to consumers for reporting and analysis.

Azure Synapse Analytics

Azure Synapse Analytics adds value throughout the data engineering lifecycle. A PaaS offering, Azure Synapse Pipelines enables developers to ingest and transform data at scale using visual workflows, using in-built Apache Spark Big Data tooling.

Synapse SQL is a massively parallel processing (MPP) cluster based on SQL server technology. This service assists with the data transformation process via SQL queries, and can also store the data as well as making it available to your end-users for access via reporting and analysis tooling. Synapse SQL can be used in one of two ways - SQL pools, dedicated resources for peak performance, or SQL on-demand, which is priced per TB processed.

All Synapse features are presented to developers from the Synapse Studio, making the process of ingesting, transforming, storing, and serving Big Data much simpler. Azure Synapse Analytics is also well integrated with Azure Data Lake storage.

Azure HDInsight

Azure HDInsight also works across the whole Big Data engineering lifecycle, much like Synapse Analytics – from data ingestion, through transformation and storage to making the data available to client, using Big Data Clusters. Also, like Synapse, it is a PaaS Azure service.

Many different cluster types are available including Apache Hadoop, Spark, and Kafka as well as many others. Azure HDInsight enables you to leverage the right open-source Big Data option, and run it in the cloud. It is possible to use different technologies in combination to cover the full Big Data development cycle.

Azure Databricks

Last up in the Azure Big Data section, we come to Azure Databricks. Azure Databricks is similar to HDInsight, but the clusters built with it are always and only Apache Spark, and the focus of the service is the data transformation phase of the lifecycle, at scale. In common with the other Azure Big Data service offerings, Databricks is a PaaS product.

Databricks was also designed as a collaboration tool for data scientists, enabling group management of clusters and data. A unified workspace which integrates well with all common Azure data services.

Azure Big Data Summary

In this section we learned about Big Data as a concept, and the development lifecycle of data science. We also learned about the Azure services that are focused on Big Data.

Azure Synapse Analytics is a modern workspace for enterprise data warehousing and analytics. It has many integrated tools like Data Factory, SQL, and Apache Spark.

Azure HDInsight is a fully managed analytics service, focused on open-source product hosting and compatible with a broad range of tools including Apache Hadoop, Spark, Kafka, and many more.

Finally Azure Databricks, which is an Apache Spark driven analytics platform for data transformation, as well as collaborative management and analysis.

Artificial Intelligence (AI) on Azure

Machine learning and AI are hot technologies right now, with a serious skills shortage in that space, especially in the cloud. The Azure Fundamentals exam requires that you possess the skills to:

Describe the benefits, and use of:

- Azure Machine Learning Service
- Azure Machine Learning Studio

Before we get into the specifics of the Azure AI service offering, a brief overview of AI. Artificial Intelligence (AI) is the branch of computing that deals with the simulation of human intelligence and human capabilities via computer software.

This is a distinct discipline to Machine Learning, which is a subcategory of AI where computer software mimics the human capacity to learn autonomously by drawing conclusions from the data made available to it and is then able to make predictions based on conclusions previously drawn. The process of teaching software to make those predictions is referred to as 'building a model'.

Azure Machine Learning

The key service for building Machine Learning models is Azure Machine Learning. The process for model development sees a model trained based on new data, that training development is then packaged and validated, before being deployed subject to satisfactory validation results. Once the model has been deployed its efficacy will be monitored, before any lessons learned from that deployment are fed back into the beginning of the process again for the next iteration, retraining the model again for continuously improving results.

Azure Machine Learning can help us with the whole lifecycle, by providing notebooks written in Python or R, as well as a visual designer which enables the build of machine learning models via a drag and drop interface in a web browser. Azure Machine Learning also provides an interface from which to manage the compute resources used to package, validate, deploy, and monitor the models, saving the effort of building compute resources separately for the purpose.

Azure Machine Learning also includes a service called Auto ML, which provides a means to deploy random algorithms at the source data to see which scores best, before deploying that version of the model. Pipelines are also included for the end-to-end build of machine learning models.

Azure Machine Learning Studio

Machine Learning Studio is a browser-based interface for managing the whole process of building, packaging, validating, deploying, and monitoring a model. Notebooks give the opportunity to test your scripts or use some of those made available from Microsoft's library to build your Machine learning model by following the tutorial and executing the sample code.

Auto ML is another option here, using randomly generating algorithms against source data to develop models for packaging and deployment.

Azure Machine Learning Studio also includes a rich asset-management function, enabling you to track components, data sources and pipelines across multiple iterations of your models.

Azure Machine Learning Summary

Azure Machine learning is a cloud-based platform for the creation, packaging, validating, deploying, and monitoring machine learning models. It is a PaaS Azure service featuring a Machine Learning Workspace and a Machine Learning Studio for end-to-end development of Machine Learning models.

Features include notebooks, using Python and R, Auto ML which can be used to run multiple algorithms and parameters before choosing the best model. A designer function is available for drag and drop creation of machine learning models, as well as data and compute management services and deployment pipelines.

A one-stop machine learning workspace in your browser!

Azure Serverless Computing

Serverless computing is somewhat contradictory as a concept. Every compute service requires a server of some description to underpin it, the Azure technologies labelled 'serverless' are those that offer compute services to the customer without any obvious interaction with a server. Essentially, the consumption of serverless computing and services allows you to concentrate only on your application, and let Microsoft worry about the technology used to make it available.

The Azure Fundamentals AZ-900 exam requires that candidates be able to describe serverless computing as a concept, as well as the Azure products that are available for serverless computing, including:

- Azure Functions
- Logic Apps
- Event Grid

Azure Functions

We learned about Azure Functions in the compute section, but as they are a serverless technology as well we will have a re-cap here. Azure Functions is a PaaS Azure service which gives customers the ability to take small pieces of code and run them as Web applications. It is designed for nano-service architectures, and event-based applications.

The code is packaged and deployed as a Function App, and from this point we go serverless with the Function App then deployed automatically to a number of underlying server nodes, made available externally to services to communication with your App.

The underlying compute scales up and down in response to application demand, and supports many popular programming languages and frameworks, such as .NET, Java, Node.js, PowerShell, Python, and many more.

Azure Logic Apps

Azure Logic Apps are designed for the orchestration of business processes, or as integration workflows. Logic Apps allow the build of workflows using a visual interface, enabling the creation of business focused or application interaction workflows. Simple workflows as well as conditions, loops and parallel runs can be constructed, as well as any combination of. A powerful No-code application solution, run serverlessly on Azure.

Logic Apps can be triggered by Web events, emails, Office 365 interactions or other Azure processes as well as many more – there are over 200 connectors available for use as trigger points, as well as being called from within a Logic App workflow. Popular workflow outputs include Blob storage, email, the Web and SQL databases.

Event Grid

Azure Event Grid is a fully managed serverless event routing service, a messaging service for Azure services. Most common Azure services can send messages to Event Grid via a number of built-in events, with messages in the Event Grid context being known as topics.

Using the publish and subscribe model, other Azure Services can then receive the messages by subscribing to a topic. The purpose of Event Grid is to ensure messages are sent successfully to topic subscribers, and it is best suited to event-based or real-time applications.

Azure Serverless Summary

In this section we learned that no Azure compute service is literally serverless, but that the terminology relates to the abstraction of the underlying infrastructure to the point you are no longer aware of it or interact with it in any way. Azure has several serverless compute service offerings.

Azure Functions is an application development platform designed for nano-services, with many popular programming languages and frameworks available.

Azure Logic Apps is an integration service for the orchestration of business and application integration workflows.

Azure Event Grid is a messaging service for applications, using the publish and subscribe model. Azure services publish messages as topics, and receiving services subscribe to the topics. Event Grid ensure successful delivery of the messages.

All these services scale on demand, Microsoft managing the performance of each dynamically and automatically.

That's serverless!

Azure DevOps

DevOps is a set of principles that combines both software development (Dev) and infrastructure operations (Ops) into one cohesive approach to running technology services. A key element of DevOps is the shortening of the development lifecycle by provision of continuous integration and continuous deliver (CI/CD) mechanisms, whilst ensuring the quality of deliverables. Azure has tools that can support that ethos.

The Azure Fundamentals exam requirements include the ability to describe the DevOps solutions available on Microsoft Azure, most notably:

- Azure DevOps
- DevTest Labs

Azure DevOps

Azure DevOps includes many tools that support the DevOps approach to deployments.

- Boards: Enables teams to track their workload, progress, and deliverables in one place.
- Repos: Manage code repositories and versioning of products.
- Pipelines: Create automated builds and deployment processes across multiple environments.

- Artifacts: Create, share, and host packages, and deploy to CI/CD pipelines with a single click.
- Test Plans: Tracks the results of manual and automated testing, including test tool inputs.

If those features are not enough, more are available via the Azure Marketplace! Azure DevOps is an evolution of Team Foundation Server (TFS) and VSTS (Visual Studio Team Services).

Azure DevTest Labs

Azure DevTest Labs provides a workspace where developers and testers can provision virtual machines as required and on-demand, test their applications, then destroy the virtual machines created when finished. A PaaS Azure service providing a sandbox for self-managed VMs, with pre-configured OS templates and large numbers of tools and applications ready to deploy.

Custom images can be created in DevTest Labs for sharing and automation. DevTest Labs includes premade plugins, APIs, and tools for CI/CD pipeline automation.

To help keep costs under control, Admins can create policies to control the operating systems available, as well as virtual machine specs and quotas to set limits on how many VMs each user can create in Azure DevTest Labs.

Azure DevOps Service Summary

A short section, in which we covered the elements required for the AZ-900 exam pertaining to DevOps, namely the introduction of the two Azure services focused on the DevOps methodology.

Azure DevOps is an end-to-end solution for building CI/CD pipelines, tracking projects and artifacts as well as managing project deliverables and code versioning.

Azure DevTest Labs is a cloud-based environment for developers and testers to create sandbox environments, build VMs with templates, with administrators creating policies to manage related costs.

Azure Management Tools

There are several ways to interact with Azure resources, and the Azure Fundamentals exam requires that you be able to describe the available tools, including:

- Azure Portal
- Azure PowerShell
- Azure CLI
- Azure Cloud Shell

Azure Portal

The Azure Portal is accessed by pointing your web browser at portal.azure.com – likely the way you have been interacting with Azure services up until now! You can manage your VMs, SQL instances, Web Apps, Network components and... everything! Well, almost everything – some 99% of Azure tasks can be completed via the portal.

It is designed for self-service, includes customizable dashboards for your convenience, and is set up for the completion of simple tasks, with help material available in line. Larger deployments and automation tasks are better handled by other tools, but Azure Portal is a good fit for the majority of use cases.

Azure PowerShell

Azure PowerShell is the first piece of tooling we have come across that is designed for automation and more complex deployments. PowerShell modules are installed on Windows client systems by default but are also available for Linux and Mac-OS devices. Once installed, it is possible to interact with your Azure subscription and services via a command terminal session.

PowerShell is simple to use, though entire books are devoted to it. One of the most helpful features of PowerShell is its contextual help – it is possible to get from almost nothing to a fully featured command line with repeated use of '/?' to guide you on the way. Some example commands include:

- Connect-AZAccount – Log in to Azure
- Get-AzResourceGroup – List resource groups
- New-AzResourceGroup – Create a resource group
- New-AzVm – Create a new Virtual Machine

And even those initial commands give an indication of syntax – relatively plain English for a scripting language! PowerShell is likely to be pretty intuitive, particularly for those with a Windows operating system background or familiarity.

Azure CLI

The Azure Command Line Interface (CLI) is more likely to appeal to those with a Linux background. Much like PowerShell, the Azure CLI tools are downloadable for Windows, Linux, and Mac-OS operating systems, and plug in to existing command terminal interfaces.

The Azure CLI, like PowerShell, is designed for automation and it is based on Python, so is fully Multi-platform. The CLI allows native OS terminal scripting, with another set of easy to use commands:

- Az login – Login to Azure
- Az group list – List resource groups
- Az group create – Create a resource group
- Az vm create – create a virtual machine

As you can see, there are consistencies in the CLI toolset that make adopting it straight forward. You can also see some similarity with Azure PowerShell.

Azure Cloud Shell

Unlike the PowerShell and CLI tooling options, which require client installation, Azure Cloud Shell provides access to Azure resources via a terminal window that runs in your web browser, using tools installed on shell.azure.com. Azure

Cloud Shell runs in an Ubuntu container, and thus provides many native Linux tools as well.

Choice of tooling is a matter of personal preference since there are distinct similarities between the three command line options. Azure Cloud Shell has some advantages:

- Microsoft managed, and always up to date.
- No client-side installation necessary
- Available via a standard web browser and can be integrated with the Azure Portal for a single management window.
- Mobile app available, for situations where a traditional desktop is not suitable.
- Supports PowerShell and the Azure CLI.
- Dozens of additional tools are available.

Azure Management Tools Summary

It is likely you will choose the Azure Portal, at least initially, as it is the most accessible interface to begin your Azure journey with. Once you need to start automating your deployments, or scripting your interactions with Azure, the tool best suited to you is largely a matter of personal preference:

Azure Portal – A web-based platform for management of Azure resources.

Azure PowerShell – A command line extension for Azure management, with a Windows-centric command syntax.

Azure CLI – A command line extension for Azure management, with a Linux-centric command syntax.

Azure Cloud Shell – A cloud-based scripting environment, with both PowerShell and CLI integrations, available from a web browser, command window or mobile app.

Azure Advisor

A quick section, as the Azure Fundamentals AZ-900 exam requires that candidates be able to describe the Azure Advisor service.

When building Azure services, it is possible to log in to the Azure Portal and spin up a number of technologies any way you like, but doing so may not necessarily give you the best result from the components you have chosen. This is where Azure Advisor comes in.

Azure Advisor can examine your technology deployments, and make recommendations to reduce cost, improve performance and reliability, improve security posture, and adhere to operational excellence – ensuring your Azure deployment is as efficient, secure, and cost-effective as possible. Azure Advisor recommendations can be sent to any interested party, with automatic notifications available as new recommendations are offered.

The best feature of Azure Advisor is the ability to act on recommendations easily. The main dashboard will display recommendations, and the benefit you will receive from accepting the recommendation. By clicking through from the dashboard you can accept the recommendation and your Azure configuration will be automatically updated for you, you will only be asked to input any information necessary to complete the configuration change.

Azure Advisor is like having a Microsoft consultant available to steer you toward best practice for your Azure deployment, with recommendations tailored to your usage. It is designed to provide recommendations and guidance around Azure best practices, in the areas of:

- Cost: VM Sizes, removing idle services, recommending reserved instances, for example.
- Security: MFA Settings, vulnerabilities, agent installations etc.
- Reliability: Redundancy, soft deletion.
- Performance: VM Sizes, IO, Disk tiers.
- Operational Excellence: Service health, subscription limits.

And, as above, Azure Advisor will provide recommendations you can action straight from the console, as well as automatically notifying you when new recommendations are made.

Exam Objective 3 – Security, Privacy, Compliance & Trust in Azure

In this section we will learn about Azure Security, Privacy, Compliance and Trust in Azure - satisfying objective three of the exam requirements, to be able to describe the building of secure applications in Azure. This subject area is worth around a third of the available marks in the exam, and security is vital to the successful deployment of services to cloud.

Azure Security Groups

In this section, we will learn about Network Security Groups (NSGs) and Application Security Groups (ASGs), satisfying the Azure Fundamentals exam objective that candidates be able to:

-   Describe Network Security Groups
-   Describe Application Security Groups

Network Security Groups

Imagine a typical Web application with database and let us say you have four web servers and a separate database server. In the real world these would exist in two separate subnets, with the data tier isolated from the Internet. In the Azure world we would accomplish the same thing using subnets, with all the systems existing within a VNet, as we covered earlier.

In the above scenario, without additional steps being taken, all traffic from the Internet would be permitted to reach all servers, and all traffic between servers within a VNet would also be permitted. This is likely not what you would want.

Think of a Network Security Group like a firewall. Network Security Groups can be linked to subnets and Virtual Machine network cards (NICs). By creating a suitable set of rules, it is possible to restrict access to systems to application specific ports, and/or restrict communications to specific systems. So, in the example above you might create NSGs as follows:

- NSG1, linked to the Web tier subnet, and permitting port 80 (HTTP) and port 443 (HTTPS) traffic for all source addresses.
- NSG1 might also include an RDP rule for port 3389 or an SSH rule on port 22, for specific support user subnets.
- NSG 2, linked to the data tier subnet, could be configured to only permit SQL traffic on port 1433 from the Web server subnet.

And in so doing, you have restricted traffic to both tiers of your application, and massively improved the security position of the overall system. The above is imperfect, but it is a good start!

NSG rules can be created to permit or block traffic from Any IP, from a specific source IP address or range, from a Service Tag within your Azure subscription, or from an Application Security Group (ASG) which we will cover soon.

After selecting a source for your rule, select a destination, port and protocol and an action – allow or deny.

NSG rules are processed in priority order, and that priority is expressed numerically – the lower the number, the higher up in the sequence a rule is processed, so a rule permitting any traffic on any port to pass with a ;priority of 100 would be processed before a rule with priority of 200 configured to allow on traffic on port 443, and using that as an example the 200 rule permitting HHTPS traffic would be pointless, since all traffic has already been allowed by the 100 rule permitting everything. Priority must be between 100 and 4096.

Finally, give you rule a name, and you are good to go. Multiple inbound and outbound rules can be configured within a Network Security Group, to control network access as tightly as required or desired.

Application Security Groups

Application Security Groups (ASGs) simplify the administration of network security in Azure. In the example used previously of a Web application with database, the NSG rules created would need to reference specific web server IP addresses for maximum security, possibly even calling for separate rules per device in some cases, and greatly increasing the complexity of the solution.

By grouping servers by function into Application Security Groups, only one set of rules is required for each group – NSG rules can be configured using the Application Security Group as the source and/or destination, instead of a specific IP address.

Azure Security Groups Summary

In this section we learned about Network Security Groups (NSGs) which work similarly to firewalls and allow the filtering of incoming and outgoing network traffic to your Azure resources.

We also learned that Application Security Groups (ASGs) can be used to simplify the creation of NSG rules, by grouping resources by type, then using those groups instead of specific IP addresses in the source and destination of the rules.

User Defined Routing

Network routing is the process of selecting or finding a path for network traffic, across one or more networks.

In Azure by default, subnets within a VNet can communicate with each other, and a route to the Internet is also created by default. If you wish to modify this behavior, you will need a user-defined route.

For example, you have created a separate network security subnet in your VNet and have a virtual firewall appliance within it. A user-defined route can be created to direct all Internet traffic from your server subnets to the firewall, which can then forward it on to the Internet. Likewise, a second user defined route could be created for the firewall to direct all authentication traffic to a third-party directory service.

User Defined Routes are easy to create, requiring a name, the destination address you wish to override the default route for, and the 'Next Hop' – which is the address traffic should be sent to for the specified destination. Once created, routes can be re-used by associating them with multiple subnets as required.

Azure Firewall

Another short section, satisfying the Azure Fundamentals requirement that candidates be able to describe Azure Firewall.

So, what is a firewall? A firewall is a network security service that allows the monitoring and control of incoming and ongoing network traffic. Some firewalls can also inspect the traffic as it passes.

Azure Firewall is a PaaS managed service that provides a virtual firewall. In the scenario we used in the previous section, the virtual firewall appliance we used for user defined routing could be an Azure Firewall.

Rules can be created on the Azure Firewall based on source, destination, port, and protocol.

Azure Firewall is a high-availability and scalable service, which supports FDQNs – Fully Qualified Domain Names, such as microsoft.com. It also integrates with Azure monitor for logging and analysis.

Azure DDoS Protection

A short section on Azure DDoS Protection, meeting the requirement that AZ-900 Azure Fundamentals exam candidates be able to describe the DDoS protection services available in Microsoft Azure.

Denial of Service (DoS) is a type of cyber attack intended to disrupt an Internet connected service, usually by flooding it with connections. A denial of service attack from a single source is easy to prevent, simply by blocking the originating IP address. For this reason, attackers will typically use a Distributed Denial of Service (DDoS) attack, which is executed from many different sources simultaneously, making it much harder to stop – especially when the malicious connections are mixed with those of legitimate users.

This is where Azure DDoS Protection comes in. The free tier of the service is readily available for deployment in front of your Azure services, and it can filter out malicious connection attempts while allowing legitimate user traffic to pass untouched.

Simply create an Azure DDoS Protection plan, and add the resources to it that you wish to protect. When associated with a VNet, everything within that VNet will be protected, preventing any additional cots for auto-scaling environments.

There are two tiers of Azure DDoS Protection:

- Basic: Automatically enabled for the Azure Platform, just create a Plan and add your resources.
- Standard: Additional mitigation and monitoring capabilities.

The Standard tier uses machine learning to analyse network patterns and improve accuracy.

Azure Identity Services

Management of user access to Azure is one of the most fundamental components of establishing a secure Azure environment. Whether you are a manager, architect, developer or administrator, an appreciation of identity is vital to your success in deploying services to the cloud.

The Azure Fundamentals exam requires that candidates be able to:

- Describe Identity, Authentication and Authorisation.
- Describe Azure Active Directory.
- Describe Multi-Factor Authentication (MFA)

Identity

Identity is what you are, in Azure terms a user with a password or an application, server or service with secret keys or certificates.

Authentication

Authentication is the process of verifying identity, by checking a password in the case of a user, or a secret key or certificate in the case of an application, server, or service.

Authorisation

Authorisation is the process of ensuring that only authenticated identities can access the resources for which they have been granted access.

Access Management

Access Management is the process of controlling, verifying, tracking, and managing access to authorized users and applications.

Azure Active Directory

Azure Active Directory (AAD) is the identity and access management solution for Azure, where users are created and passwords stored, that then authenticates users and authorizes their access to Azure resources. All out interactions with Azure require permission be granted via Azure Active Directory. Azure Active Directory manages users, groups, and applications, as well as access to Azure subscriptions, resource groups, roles, and role assignments.

Azure AD also manages access to Microsoft's SaaS products, such as Skype, Outlook, Live mail, and OneDrive. Azure AD also manages access to Office 365 applications and services.

Azure Active Directory synchronises with on-prem Active Directory via sync services.

Multi-Factor Authentication

As computers become ever-more powerful passwords become easier to crack, and as more and more of our lives move online, so those passwords become more accessible as well as vital for daily life. Multi-Factor Authentication (MFA)strengthens the security of passwords by introducing another hurdle for the authentication process.

MFA can be thought of authentication using more than one thing (or factor) to establish you are who you say you are. Typically, this will take the form of providing two or more of the following:

- Something you know, such as a password.
- Something you have, which could be a key fob smart card token, a mobile device that a code is sent to, or similar physical item.
- Something you are – your fingerprint, voice, facial recognition etc.
- Somewhere you are – GPS or network location.

MFA is supported by Azure Active Directory, just switch it on.

Azure Security Center

Azure Security Center is responsible for continuously scanning your Azure services, be they PaaS or IaaS – Virtual Machines, SQL Databases, Web services and so on, helping to protect your Azure environment.

Azure Security Center automatically generates recommendations and notifies Azure Administrators, enabling rapid remediation of any issues to maintain a secure environment. The security recommendations offered by Azure Advisor are actually created by Azure Security Center.

Azure Security Center can be extended to your on-prem systems with the installation of client software, enabling the same protections for your on-prem infrastructure as within Azure.

Azure Security Center provides an overview of security posture, divided into easy to navigate sub-sections:

- Outstanding recommendations and security alerts.
- Your Azure subscription will be given a secure score automatically, the higher the number the more secure your environment is.
- The insights section displays the highest priority recommendations, which are those you should focus on first.
- Azure Defender is the paid-for version of Security Center, which includes more in-

depth analysis, Just In Time (JIT) access and threat detection tooling. JIT is the ability to only permit RDP access to a server on a time-limited basis. Azure Defender is modular and priced on a consumption model, so only switch it on for the resources requiring the enhanced service.

- The regulatory compliance section uses popular regulatory frameworks such as SOC, ISO 27001 and PCI DSS, and tracks your adherence to their requirements. Helpful in regulated environments.

- The Inventory provides a high-level overview of your Azure resources, and their security status.

Much like Azure Advisor, recommendations, the recommendations of Azure Security Center can be actioned direct from the dashboard.

Azure Security Center is embedded in many Azure services, meaning the recommendations for security improvements to services are available from within those services directly, as well as via Security Center itself.

Azure Key Vault

Azure Key Vault is the service used for securely storing application identity artifacts such as passwords, keys, and certificates. The Azure Fundamentals exam requires that candidates be able to describe Azure Key Vault, and have an appreciation for how it can be used.

To demonstrate use of Azure Key Vault, we will look at three scenarios, and see how Key Vault can be deployed in each.

1. Virtual Machine Disks: By default, disks for Virtual Machines are encrypted using Azure managed keys. If the customer decides they wish to manage the encryption keys themselves, they can generate a new key to decrypt the drive, and that key can be stored in Azure Key Vault, with the virtual machine granted access to the key. IN this way the Virtual Machine can decrypt the disk on demand.

2. Application Access: A Web application would need connectivity information to connect to a SQL database, namely a server address as well as a username and password. Saving that information on the Web server introduces the possibility of compromise, and it is much safer to store it as an application secret in Key Vault, which can be retrieved on demand by the Web application only.

3. Secure Communications: Web servers sending content over encrypted

channels to client systems need certificates to secure those communications, just as service authentication can be configured to use certificates. In both cases, the certificates can be stored in Azure Key Vault.

Three examples, showing the three main purposes of Key Vault – the storage of Keys, Secrets and Certificates.

Secrets can be created to activate at a specific date and time, or to expire at a specific date and time. Each has a version number, and when a secret is updated, all older versions of that secret become obsolete. Key Vault is a PaaS managed service for storing sensitive information sets, and it is integrated with many other Azure services including VMs, Logic Apps, Web Apps and Data Factory.

All access to Azure Key Vault is monitored and Logged.

Role-Based Access Control

Rather than assign Azure permissions to users on an individual basis, which is time-consuming, difficult to control and introduces the possibility of inconsistency, the preferred method is role-based access control. This means that a set of permissions are associated with a role, which can then be assigned to an identity to grant those permissions. The user account, group or service is known as a Security Principal.

A Security Principal is an Azure object or Identity, which can be assigned a role – such as a user, group, or application.

For example, an 'Office Administrator' role could be created, and permissions to reset user passwords, create new users and access departmental Virtual Machines granted. When a new staff member joins, adding them to the role will be the single step required to ensure they have all the Azure access they need to perform their duties. When they leave the department, those same rights can be revoked quickly and easily by removing the role from their user account.

A role can be allocated to any security principal in Azure, usually one of the following:

- A User
- A Group (collection of users)
- A Service Principal (Application Accounts)

- A Managed Identity (Application Account tied to a specific service)

It is common to assign multiple roles to a security principal to permit them to access the systems and services they need to, whilst using a principle known as 'least privilege', which is to grant the minimum permissions necessary to a security principal to achieve the required task.

Roles also have a scope, which controls the boundary of permissions granted. Azure is hierarchical, and Management Groups are at the top of the structure – roles assigned at the Management Group level will see their permissions cascade down through all subscriptions, resource groups and resources beneath. It is likely you will have a subscription at the top of your structure. A Security Principal granted permission at subscription level would have the same permissions in all the resource groups and resources within that subscription, whilst a role granting permission at resource group level, would be restricted to resources within that specific resource group. Roles can also be set with resource specific scope assignments, though doing so increases admin overhead significantly.

Role-based Access Control Summary

Role-based Access Control (RBAC) is an authorization system built on Azure Resource Manager (ARM). It is designed for the granular management of Azure resources by role.

Role assignment is a combination of:

- Role definition, which dictates the permissions and access types granted – creating VMs, deleting accounts, modifying SQL databases etc.
- Security Principals, which are users, groups, service principals and managed identities.
- Scope, which dictates whether the permissions granted to the security principal are limited to a resource, resource group, subscription, or management group.

Scope is hierarchical, so a role assigned to one of the scopes below will see the same permissions granted to all subordinate structures, show to its left:

Management Group > Subscription > Resource Group > Resources

Azure RBAC supports Built-in roles designed by Microsoft for common usage scenarios, as well as custom roles created for bespoke requirements.

Azure Resource Locks

Granting users permissions in Azure is already a nice granular process, enabling fine control over who can do what with your cloud services. You should only assign high level permissions to trusted staff, preferably those in possession of Azure skills and experience.

Users with the 'Owner' role in Azure are empowered to do just about anything within a subscription, so that permission should be restricted to as few people as possible. An Owner can:

- Read
- Create
- Update
- Delete

And if he deletes a virtual machine by accident, that could create a problem. Recover from backup, sure, but that backup may be several hours or even days old. Problem!

Azure Resource Locks provide the ability to control access to resources, with two options available:

- Delete Lock: Leaves all other user permissions intact but prevents the deletion of an object unless/until the lock is removed.
- Read-only Lock: Restricts all permissions that alter the state of an Azure resource, making 'Read' the only available option.

Using these locks can prevent accidental deletion or modification of Azure resources, whilst maintaining all existing roles and privileges.

Resource Locks can be managed at an individual resource level, or at a subscription level, but applying them at resource group level is a better balance of effectiveness against administrative overhead. When a Resource Lock is applied at the resource group level, it is enforced on all resources within the group.

Resource Locks cannot be applied at the Management Group level.

Production systems holding customer data are a popular use case for Azure Resource locks, to safeguard the live services and the integrity of the data.

Only the Owner and User Access Administrator built-in roles can manage Resource Locks.

Azure Resource Tags

As we learned previously, Azure Resource Groups can be used to band Azure resources together, popularly by application, environment, department and so on. But a resource can only exist in one resource group and no matter how good your strategy for resource grouping, it is likely to need to change over time.

Organisations change – departments change, bill payers change, application services restructure. All of these could drive the recreation of resource groups, or confuse the strategy initially chosen.

Resource tags are a compliment to resource groups, in so far as they give you the opportunity to create attributes for your resources. A simple Key / Value pair. You might create tags for owner, department, cost centre, application, and primary function – a resource can have many associated tags.

Doing this would mean the ability to search your Azure services for particular tags, attribute all resources belonging to a department to a cost centre when paying the bill, even managing all resources with a specific tag at the same time. Security, automation, and operations can be completed using Resource Tags. Billing remains the primary use case for Resource Tags – use Tags for cost centre, and use them to split the bill within your organisation.

Resource tags are not inherited by default, so a Resource Tag applied to a resource group would not apply to the resources within that group, though that can be achieved using Azure Policy.

Azure Policy

Azure Policy is one of the main aspects of Azure Governance, and the Azure Fundamentals exam requires that candidates be equipped to describe the functionality and usage of Azure Policy.

When creating Azure resources, we choose the properties associated with the resource we intend to create – Type, Location, and SKU for example. Azure will validate this request in terms of it being a properly formed request from an authorized identity before submission to the resource manager for creation in line with the configuration options specified. The final check made before creation of the resource is against Azure Policy.

So, what is Azure Policy? Think of it as a set of guard rails that control what you can create in Azure. I work with customers in Government and other regulated environments, and let us say that each customer is obliged by regulation or legislation to store data within a specific geographical location only. Without Azure Policy, an admin could create a virtual machine on the other side of the world, and the orgnaisation could be in breach of its obligations, probably without even knowing. By using Azure Policy to specify that virtual machines may only be created in a subscription within US geographical regions, we can prevent machines being created anywhere else, automatically and consistently.

Azure Policy is designed to help with resource governance, security, compliance, and cost management, and they focus on resource properties. There are a large number of built-in policies in Azure, ready to use with just a few clicks.

Use of Azure Policy presents another opportunity to exercise granular control over your deployments, and prevent individuals with otherwise high levels of privilege from deploying resources in ways other than those specified in policy.

Azure Blueprints

Azure Blueprints are our last stop in the section of this book discussing Azure Governance. The AZ-900 exam syllabus requires that candidates be able to describe the functionality and use of Azure Blueprints.

An Azure Blueprint is a guide, pattern, or design for creating Azure resources, ensuring consistency. Using the example of typical Web application with SQL database backend, you would likely find yourself creating a number of Azure resources to support it – including the following:

- Resource Group
- Web Server
- SQL Database
- Policy Assignments (location, resource tags)
- Role Assignments

And it is likely to become more work as time passes and more standards are adopted by your organization. To save the admin overhead, all these Azure components can be bundled up into an Azure Blueprint definition. When you assign the blueprint for deployment, Azure will deploy all resources and settings within a blueprint, automatically. And a blueprint can be used as many times as required.

Many built-in blueprint definitions are available, covering popular technologies, stacks, and regulatory frameworks.

For the exam, remember that Azure Blueprints offer centralized storage for organizationally approved design patterns. That blueprint definitions describe what should be deployed, as a reusable package. Blueprint assignments describe where the blueprint should be deployed.

Cloud Adoption Framework

This section deals with the Cloud Adoption Framework, as it relates to the Microsoft Azure platform. As ever, the AZ-900 Azure Fundamentals exam requires that you be able to describe the Cloud Adoption Framework, with reference to Microsoft Azure.

What is Cloud Adoption?

The clue is in the title on this one – Cloud Adoption is the strategic decision by an organization to leverage cloud in their business model – usually to reduce costs whilst maximizing performance, availability, and agility, thereby providing better value to customers.

The Cloud Adoption Framework for Azure is a collection of tools, best practices, guidelines, and documents created by Microsoft to guide organisations in their journey to the cloud. There is an enormous amount of information in the Cloud Adoption Framework for Azure, but thankfully you only need a familiarity with it for the purposes of the Azure Fundamentals exam – so this section is a high-level summary.

Phase 1 – Strategy

The first phase of the Cloud Adoption Framework for Azure deals with the alignment or organizational strategy in readiness for a move to cloud.

The first step is to establish motivations for cloud, and articulating these with your key stakeholders. These motivations are likely to be driven by the cost savings and efficiencies of a migration to cloud, or the opportunities for innovation in the cloud in the form of global scale, product transformation or market disruption.

Next up is the definition of business outcomes associated with a move to cloud, and how to quantify success against the measure. Common targeted outcomes include increases in revenue or profit, reductions in cost or exploitation of new markets.

Step three of phase one is the development of a business case to validate the financial model supporting the business case for the adoption of cloud, informed by the outcomes of the two previous steps. Microsoft provide several tools to help with cloud cost estimation, including:

- The Azure TCO Calculator
- The Azure Pricing Calculator
- Azure Cost Management

Finally in the first phase of cloud adoption, it is recommended an organization choose a first project, to provide justification for initial costs and to focus technical capabilities. The criteria used to identify a suitable first project candidate are:

- It should be an already running service with a dedicated owner.
- The owner should have motivation to move, having acknowledged the advantages of cloud.
- The technology underpinning the project should have minimal dependencies and existing physical assets.

A small and self-contained project is recommended to allow rapid completion, enabling validation of the overall strategy.

Phase 2 – Plan

The second phase of the Cloud Adoption Framework for Azure deals with planning, an inventory of assets and the digital estate.

Each project should be evaluated with the so-called "Five R's of Rationalisation" in mind:

- Rehost: A virtual lift and shift of existing assets to the cloud – typically an IaaS Virtual Machine-driven exercise.
- Refactor: Modest technical change to fit existing applications in to Azure PaaS offerings.
- Re-Architect: More complex changes to application code to take advantage of new Azure services. May also be the best approach when existing code relies heavily on existing physical infrastructure.

- Rebuild: Applications recreated from scratch in response to a large amount of legacy technology, or unnecessary complexity.
- Replace: Evaluating whether whole services can be replaced with native cloud equivalents, Office 365 to succeed existing productivity and messaging services, for example.

Once each project has been aligned with an approach, initial alignment with stakeholders can commence. Assignment of technical resources to projects can also happen at this stage, as well as planning to cover any gaps in skills.

Phase 3 – Ready

Following the strategy and planning phases, phase three of the Cloud Adoption Framework for Azure is the preparation of your organisation's first Azure environment.

Microsoft provide guidance and documentation to support this piece of decision making, and once key decisions around Azure subscriptions have been taken an initial Azure environment, referred to as a Landing Zone, can be created. This will be your organisation's first Azure environment, built in-line with Microsoft's best practice. Ideally infrastructure as code will be developed and deployed, building consistency and scalability from the very beginning.

The initial Landing Zone can be extended to support the requirements and aspirations of your organization. It is important to repeatedly refer to Microsoft best practices as you expand into Azure to avoid creating a poorly designed Azure environment, which will be difficult to redesign once launched.

Phase 4 – Adopt

Once ready to consume Azure services, adoption is the logical final step in the Cloud Adoption Framework for Azure. Once again, we have a number of stages to work through, some of which have been touched upon in previous sections.

Once you work through your first migration, you can use the lessons learned in that exercise to inform future migration scenarios, avoiding pitfalls organizationally or in terms of technology transition. By establishing your own best practices, building on those provided by Microsoft, you can identify improvements and become incrementally more efficient in terms of time, resource consumption and cost, as you work through your transit to cloud.

The innovation side of cloud adoption begins with what Microsoft call a business value consensus, which means to map a customer need to an established value, which can in turn be mapped to a technology solution fulfilled by your cloud strategy. From there, we move to the innovation guide, which helps us identify tools that can be used to accelerate our development and transformation into cloud. This will guide us in creating a minimum viable product (MVP), the innovation equivalent of a 'first project' for migration – from this initial undertaking we can learn lessons and become incrementally more efficient in cloud innovation.

Adherence to bets practice is as important in innovation as it is in migration, and a solid foundation is much more dependable as a starting point than an incoherent strategy cobbled together as you go. Each product iteration should seek feedback from users and stakeholders, driving continuous improvement both in product and process. Once again becoming more efficient in terms of time, cost, and resource consumption. As well as building ever more elegant solutions in the cloud.

Although the Cloud Adoption Framework for Azure is a four-stage process, it is the Plan, Ready, and Adopt stages that shape an organisation's embrace of cloud. If in the exam you are asked what the three stages of the Cloud Adoption Framework for Azure are, the answer you are being asked for is:

- Plan
- Ready
- Adopt

The other stages we speak of hear support the core trifecta of the framework. The final two stages run consecutively and in parallel with

Plan, Ready and Adopt – and are Govern and Manage.

Govern and Manage

The Govern stage mandates that we define governance solutions for our organization, in terms of business need, agility and risk management / mitigation. It ensures compliance with regulatory frameworks, control over deployments and transformations, and security by design.

From there we move toward the Manage stage, which emphasizes the importance of stability and cost control in meeting business commitments. The Manage stage helps guide us toward best practice in operations and service optimization.

Microsoft provide an enormous amount of documentation in support of the Cloud Adoption Framework for Azure. The structures, stages and processes are laid out clearly, hopefully as they are previously, but in greater detail with a large volume of documents and reference architectures for you to seek inspiration from as required.

Documentation and communication are critical at every stage of this process.

Security, Privacy and Compliance – Core Tenets

The Azure Fundamentals requirement to describe the purpose of the Security, Privacy and Compliance Core Tenets specifies that candidates should be familiar with the Microsoft key documents and websites underpinning the Azure platform, including the Privacy Statement, Service Terms, Data Protection Addendum, Trust Center, and Azure Compliance Documentation. Candidates should also understand the purpose of specialist Azure regions for Azure Government and Azure China.

Privacy Statement

The Privacy Statement is similar to many others you will have seen, in so far as it details the personal data Microsoft collect, the purpose for that collection, and the circumstances in which the data collected may be sued.

This is framed in terms of the services, applications, websites, products, software, and devices Microsoft offer.

This document is designed for all consumers of Microsoft services,

Online Services Terms (OST)

This document is a legal agreement between Microsoft and the user, and details the licensing terms for consumption of online services such as Azure, Office 365, Dynamics 365. This document describes what is permitted or prohibited in the usage of the online services.

This document is designed for a legal audience.

Data Protection Addendum (DPA)

The data protection addendum details the obligations both Microsoft and your organization have when it comes to the processing and safeguarding of personal and customer data.

This document is an addendum to the OST, so the content is framed in terms of Microsoft's online services. It is designed for legal and security teams primarily.

Trust Center

Trust Center is a website run by Microsoft, which includes all information and policies related to Microsoft online services. This helps businesses to understand what they can trust Microsoft with their business-critical services and data. Trust Center includes the following information:

- Security
- Compliance
- Privacy
- Policy
- Practice

As they relate to Microsoft online services such as Azure, Dynamics and Office 365. The information begins at a high level, but you can drill down to the detail in each specific topic.

Azure Compliance Documentation

This portal offers information specifically around Azure compliance, using a similar structure to the compliance section of Trust Center, with everything being Azure-specific.

Compliance information is sorted in to National, US Government, Industry-specific and Regional sections, to help you find that most relevant to you.

Azure Sovereign Regions

We have already covered Azure Regions, there are many spread all around the world. These are Public Cloud Regions. In addition to these, there are two regions dedicated for specific purposes.

The US Government Region is a dedicated Azure Region only accessible to US Government agencies and their contractors or authorized partners. The region is entirely US-based but based in locations across the US – a separate instance and separate portal to access it. It is also physically isolated, though most Azure services are available.

The qualifying criteria for access are strict, and vetting is comprehensive. This helps achieve a higher security benchmark as mandated by the US Government.

Azure China is similar in setup to Azure US Government, but set up for the regulatory requirements of China – specifically that if you wish to operate cloud services in China, you need to be a registered telecoms provider with less than 50% foreign interest. Microsoft cannot meet this requirement as an international company, so a separate Azure region was created to meet the specific regulatory framework in China. It is operated by a separate company – 21 Vianet.

Exam Objective 4 – Azure pricing, service level agreements and support

In this section we will learn about Azure pricing, service level agreements (SLA), and support - satisfying objective four of the exam requirements, to be able to describe the structure of Azure pricing, as well as the support you and your organization can expect from Microsoft when building and operating applications and in Azure. This subject area is worth up to a quarter of the available marks in the exam, and understanding costs and support models is vital to the successful deployment of services to cloud.

Azure Pricing

In this section, we will learn about the purchasing of Azure services, and consider the factors that impact the cost of building in the cloud.

A good start to calculating Azure costs is the Total Cost of Ownership calculator we have covered previously, but it is important to understand how costs are generated in Azure so you can understand how your design decisions affect the bottom-line, as well as how and where savings can be made for your organization.

Azure Account Subscriptions

Microsoft offer several subscription tiers which underpin the charging structure:

- Free: An introductory offer from Microsoft providing 12 months of free access to popular services, as well as an account credit you can use to explore Azure services for 30 days – ideal for Azure certification study! Any services you build will expire at the end of the trial period, or when your credit expires, unless you switch toa paid subscription.
- Pay as you go: The traditional consumption-based charging model where you pay for what you use. Organisations can apply for volume discounts and pre-paid invoicing.
- Member offers: Other Microsoft subscriptions offer credits for your Azure account, Visual Studio subscriptions and Microsoft Partner Network being notable examples.

Buying Azure Services

There are three main ways to provision Azure services. The first is the obvious one – creating an account, signing up for one of the tiers outlined in the previous section and selecting the resources you need to build your solutions. Each has a price displayed so you will know what you are getting in to before you begin. You can also return to the TCO calculator to get a view of the full stack.

Larger customers may enter into a Microsoft Enterprise Agreement, which commits them to an agreed level of send in Azure over three years in return for preferential pricing on Azure products and services.

The final option here would be to use a partner company to build Azure services on your behalf. A Cloud Solution Provider (CSP) can build your Azure resources and bill you for them directly, so you need not concern yourself with Azure billing at all. They will of course be charging you additional fees for that service!

Once you have decided how you will engage with Azure, you can start building your applications and services, underpinned by Azure resources. You select the applications and services you need and your account is billed according to the Azure consumption-based model, where you only pay for what you use. At the end of each month, you will be invoiced for the Azure resources used. You can use Azure Cost Management and Billing from the Azure

Portal to view a summary of your current usage, as well as comparing it against activity in previous months.

How is the Cost Calculated?

Many elements have an impact on Azure cost, subscription type and any pricing from intermediaries being the foundation. From there, pricing is dependent on the volume and type of resources you consume as well as how much time they are running for.

For example, Virtual Machines are available in many different types – more RAM, more CPU, faster disks, optimization for various compute-intensive operations. In simple terms, the more you need the more you pay.

When you build Azure services, Azure creates meters to track usage of those resources and enable accurate billing – similar to the meter running in a taxi – you are paying for the time you are in the Cab for your journey.

Put simply, Azure cost is calculated by multiplying the resources you provision by the time they are running, plus any service specific considerations. Using a Virtual Machine as an example, charging will be built from a calculation based on overall CPU run time, any public IP addresses assigned, network traffic in and out of the VM, disk size and the quantity of read/write operations. Most Azure services have their own equivalent of these specialist factors.

Usage

As we know, Azure has a consumption-based model. In some respects this is simple – only pay for what you use, however the reality is a little more complicated than that.

For example, a VM that is running attracts a charge as outlined previously. A VM that has been deleted attracts no charges as it has been completely removed from your Azure account. A VM that has been deallocated, however, attracts no charges for CPU time or public IP addresses but storage is retained thus charging for that storage continues.

This is a bad thing if you intended to remove the VM, and accidentally left storage as an ongoing cost, but it can also be a good thing in terms of deallocating a VM that is not required for a period of time, as costs will be minimized until it is needed again, at which point it can be quickly brought back in to service.

Location

When you provision Azure resources, you are required to define a region. Azure is global distributed, but different regions have different prices, and use of different regions versus user locations can impact traffic flows, with network traffic being one of the influences on cost. So a company choosing to locate their Azure services in a region where the resources cost the least, could see those savings eroded or overtaken by the cost of the increased network utilization. It is generally best to position Azure resources closest to their consuming users, for performance and cost.

Bandwidth & Zones

Billing zones determine the cost of some Azure services. Some data transfers into Azure are free, data transfer out of Azure data centres are priced by zone. A zone is a geographical group of Azure regions, with the following as examples:

- **Zone 1**: Australia Central, West US, East US, Canada West, West Europe, France Central, and others.
- **Zone 2**: Australia East, Japan West, Central India, Korea South, and others.
- **Zone 3**: Brazil South, South Africa North, South Africa West, UAE Central, UAE North

Estimating Cost

You can estimate your Azure costs by taking in to account all the factors covered previously in this section, and the Azure Pricing Calculator can help you in that effort. The pricing calculator displays Azure products and services by category and allows you collect the components of your solution together to be presented with an estimated cost. Those estimates can be saved for future use and amended as solutions develop.

You can tweak various aspects of your solution and review the cost impact. Some services have configuration options specific to them, with examples including:

- Region
- Tier
- Billing option
- Support options
- Offers
- Dev/Test pricing

It is important to remember that the pricing calculator provides cost estimates and not quotes. Actual prices may fluctuate depending on date of purchase, prevailing currency conversion rates and the type of account holder you are.

Cost Reduction Methods

There are many methods that may be used to deliver Azure cost efficiencies. In this section we will identify factors that can help reduce costs such as the use of reserved instances, reserved capacity, and spot pricing. We can also use the Pricing calculator and the Total Cost of Ownership (TCO) calculator discussed previously to build the most cost-effective solution available.

The TCO Calculator

Cost reduction starts with the move to cloud! The Total Cost of Ownership (TCO) Calculator helps you estimate the cost savings associated with operating your services out of Azure rather than your own data centre over the longer term.

Simply enter details of your existing servers and supporting infrastructure, and the TCP calculator will display an industry-average for related operational costs, before displaying a side-by-side comparison report to show the same workloads running in Azure.

It is a simple three-stage process where you define your existing systems, adjust any of the assumptions the calculator uses to generate operational costs and review the resulting report output. You do not even need to be an Azure customer to use the TCO Calculator!

Azure Advisor

Once you have moved your applications and services to Azure, there are still many ways to optimize costs. Start by carefully planning the products, services, and resources you need. Read all related documentation and use the Pricing Calculator to generate a cost estimate. Fine tune to deliver the most cost-effective solution possible on Azure.

Once up and running you can use the Azure Advisor to monitor your usage. Azure Advisor can identify unused or undertilised resources and recommends the removal of such products from your account. You can use Azure Advisor to help configure resources to match the workloads you are currently using.

The recommendations are displayed in impact order – high, medium, or low, based on the contribution they are making to your Azure account costs. Azure Advisor can automatically fix some underlying issues, while anything that requires human intervention prompts the account holder to take action.

Spending Limits

When using a free trial or credit-based Azure subscription, it is possible to set spending limits to prevent your bill from exceeding a specific value.

If you set a $100 a month limit, for example, once that limit is reached all billable Azure resources will be stopped, and virtual machines will be deallocated. Data remains read-only, and you can upgrade your subscription to a paid account.

Credit-based subscriptions work similarly, if you hit your monthly credit limit all your Azure resources are suspended until the next billing period.

Azure Reservations

Azure Reservations offer discounted pricing on specific Azure services, saving you up to 72% compared to the pay as you go standard pricing. To secure the discount, you simply need to reserve the Azure services you require and start paying in advance.

For example, you could pay for a virtual machine for one or three years and receive a 72% discount on the cost, but you would be tied into a contract for the full period. A good option if you are certain the resources in question will be required for the duration.

Azure reservations are available to customers with Enterprise Agreements, Cloud Solution Providers (CSPs) and pay as you go subscribers.

Cost Management & Billing Control

Azure Cost Management + Billing is a free Azure service that helps you understand your monthly bill, monitor and control Azure spend and ensure efficient use of resources. Features include:

- Reporting: Historical data used to generate reports, forecast future usage, and calculate likely expenditure.
- Data Enrichment: Catagorise resources using tags corresponding to cost centres.
- Budgets: Create and manage cost and usage budgets, monitor demand trends, consumption rates and cost patterns.
- Alerting: Configure alerts based on cost and usage thresholds.
- Recommendations: Configure and receive recommendations to optimize Azure resource use, and remove idle services.

Add Resource Tags

Ensuring you tag resources properly in Azure can help ensure accountability for Azure spend, as well as simplifying the process of distributing the costs between business units. Analysis can be run against tags to see at a glance how much is being consumed by each business unit, and Azure Policy can be used to enforce the use of tags when creating Azure resources.

Review VMs

A common recommendation from Azure Advisor is to reduce the size of underutilized virtual machines – you can typically cut the bill for a VM in half by moving down one level in VM specification. The resizing of a VM requires it be stopped, resized, and then restarted, a process that can take several minutes, so make sure you plan for this if the VM is in live service.

On a similar theme, you can deallocate virtual machines during non-business hours to minimize cost. Doing so preserves the hard disks and data, but the VM stops running, saving all cost related to CPU time. An excellent solution for development and test environments, and Azure can help you automatically start and stop your VMs on a schedule.

Delete Unused Resources

Well…. Duh! Regular review of systems to ensure you are only paying for what you need is a smart thing to do, and Azure Advisor can help identify candidates based on low levels of usage. Shutdown or remove everything that is not in use.

Migrate from IaaS to PaaS

If appropriate for your business circumstances and technical requirements, you will likely find Azure PaaS cheaper than running equivalent services on IaaS virtual machine infrastructure. Consider swapping a VM running SQL for PaaS Azure SQL and save yourself the costs associated with licensing and support of the VM, the operating system and SQL.

Reduce Licensing Costs

There are two ways Azure can reduce software licensing costs:

- Azure makes it quick and easy to provision a VM running Windows or Linux. If the application being built does not require Windows, using Linux can reduce licensing costs.
- Use Azure Hybrid to repurpose existing on-prem software licenses for use in the cloud, where possible and permitted.

So, as you can see, Azure provides many opportunities to reduce costs by migrating to cloud, building cloud services efficiently to make best use of resources, and provides tools to enable you to both control your spending, and optimize your workloads.

Make sure to tag all resources from the off and use Azure Advisor to stay on top of the monthly spend.

Azure Cost Management

Azure Cost Management provides you with the tools to plan, analyse and reduce your Azure spending to achieve best value from your cloud investment. Azure makes it easy to deploy cloud resources, but it is your responsibility to ensure efficient use of those resources. There are five key principles that drive Azure cost efficiency:

1) Planning: Establishing the business problem you are solving and the suage patterns you expect from every Azure service helps inform selection of the best fit resources.

2) Visibility: Cost Management tooling helps make costs visible to internal stakeholders, as well as identifying usage patterns and trends.

3) Accountability: Cost attribution is vital for Azure billing, and Tags help enormously in this. Good organization from the start can help ensure the consumers of the Azure resources pay for the resources they are consuming.

4) Optimisation: As introduced in the previous section, downsize VMs, switch off anything not being used, look at licensing models, and regularly review Azure Advisor recommendations.

5) Iteration: Review Azure costs regularly and seek to drive continuous improvements in your cloud services and utlisation.

Cost Management tool can be found within your subscription and resource group windows, or the Cost Management + Billing window.

Using Cost Analysis

The Cost Analysis functions within Cost Management provide several options for viewing costs and performing analysis.

-   The accumulate cost view displays all costs by date range, defaulting to the current billing period. You can use this view to track costs within a billing cycle, or costs as a percentage of budget.
-   The actual cost view shows total usage and purchase costs for the current month, as they will be displayed on your bill at the end of the billing period.
-   The forecast view displays costs to date within a billing period, as well as a forecast for the rest of the billing period based on previous usage trends. This view is useful for tracking spend against budgets and limits.
-   Budget simply displays your budget.
-   Pivot charts break down total cost by common sets of standard properties. Costs are categorized by service, location, and child scope by default.

Customised Views

The Cost Analysis tool shows data for the current month by default, and date ranges can be easily manipulated within the tool. Other useful data collation options include:

- Accumulated Costs: display all costs within a date range.
- Cost by Resource: Grouped resources sorted by highest cost.
- Daily cost: A view of costs by day. This view is designed to aid in the identification of anomalies in cost, either spikes or dips against the baseline.
- Cost by service: Shows the last three months by default, allowing easy comparison between the current three-month period, and those previous.

Saving and Sharing

One you have created a custom view in Cost Analysis, that view can be pinned to your Azure dashboard for future use and quick access. It is then possible to share your dashboard with others in your team to ensure everyone has the same view of the Azure cost data.

You can share a link to your custom view that others can use to access the data. Users with Cost Management contributor access (or greater) can create shared views, up to 50 per scope.

If you need to share a view outside your Azure organization, export charts as images and use them in emails or other documents as you require.

Reports can also be exported to an Azure Storage account – simply select the date range you require and directory path. It can take up to 24-hours before the data export runs.

Budgets and Alerts

You can create an Azure account subscription budget for the month, quarter, or year. Simply select the scope (management group or subscription) and create a new budget.

Once the budget has been set, select a threshold for alerts as a percentage o that total budget – you can create up to five thresholds and specify five different email addresses for the alert notifications. Notifications are sent within 8 hours of a budget threshold being reached.

Once created, budgets are displayed in the Cost Analysis tool for comparison with current spend.

Action Groups

When a budget is created it can be configured to call an action group, and that action group can perform a variety of actions when a threshold is met.

Cost Alerts

Cost Management supports other types of alert, and all active alerts are shown together in Cost Management + Billing. Alerts are generated when your Azure resource consumption reaches a specified threshold based on budget, cost, or departmental spending quota.

Azure Service Level Agreements

A service level agreement (SLA) is a formal agreement between Microsoft and their customers defining the performance standards Microsoft commit to offering you via their Azure platform. Understand the SLA helps you understand the availability of services offered to you, which will underpin the SLA you offer your customers for any service hosted in Azure.

Each Azure service has its own SLA. A typical SLA includes an introductory section which explains what to expect in the SLA, including scope and how service renewal ca affect terms.

The general SLA terms defines the terms of the agreement, how to submit a claim and receive credit for any performance or availability issue and the limitations of such compensation.

The SLA details are where the specific guarantees for the Azure service are defined. Availability statistics are expressed as a percentage, with 100% representing all the time. Azure commitments are typically between 99.9% (three nines) and 99.99% (four nines). The main performance metric measured is service uptime, although some services also include metrics for latency. This section will also define any additional terms specific to the Azure service in question.

Free services do not typically have an SLA, and service credits are not associated with the underperformance of any free Azure service.

How Percentages Map to Downtime

As previously explained, Azure performance metrics are usually expressed as a percentage of uptime. An availability of 99% only permits 7.2 hours of downtime per month, 99.9% moves this to 43.2 minutes of downtime per month. 99.99% would only allow for 21.6 minutes of downtime per month and by the time you get to 99.999% Microsoft can only have the service unavailable for 25.9 seconds per month before breaching their SLA! See the table below for a breakdown of the downtime per month or year associated with each popular Azure SLA.

SLA %	Downtime pcm	Downtime pa
99	7.2 hours	3.65 days
99.9	43.2 minutes	8.76 hours
99.95	21.6 minutes	4.38 hours
99.99	4.32 minutes	52.56 minutes
99.999	25.9 seconds	5.26 minutes

The downtime is cumulative, meaning the duration of multiple outages is added together for a running availability within SLA calculation.

Service Credits

Service credits are the percentage of the fees you paid for an Azure service that are credited back to you in the event of a successful claim for services falling beneath the guarantee offered by the SLA.

Credits typically increase as availability decreases, the breakdown shown below shows

how service credits are applied in the case of
Azure Database for MySQL as an example:

Monthly uptime %	Service credit %
< 99.99	10
< 99	25
< 95	100

How are outages identified?

Azure status gives a global overview of Azure
service health across regions. If you suspect an
Azure outage, Azure status is a good place to
start. You can subscribe to the RSS feed as well
as visiting the website.

The Azure status page also provides access to
Azure Service Health, which displays a
personalized view of the health of the Azure
services and regions you are using directly from
the Azure Portal.

Requesting Service Credits

Making a claim with Microsoft for service credits
is simple. If you use a Cloud Service Provider
(CSP), they will manage the process on your
behalf.

Each Azure service SLA will specify the amount
of time you have to make a claim, as well as
how long Microsoft will take to process that
claim, in most cases your claim must be made

before the end of the calendar month to which it relates.

Designing your Application

Your application or service SLA defines the performance and availability of your application or service. It cannot reasonably offer greater uptime than the SLA you receive from your supplier for the supporting infrastructure.

Your application should be designed to meet the business requirement for availability. It is likely you would like your application or service to be available all the time without exception, but some interruption to service is likely no matter what you do. There are steps you can take to improve availability, performance, and resilience, but there is a balance to be struck between availability, complexity, and cost:

- Using PaaS removes the reliance on virtual machines, and typically builds in higher availability / deployment across multiple availability zones or regions and so on.
- Use load balancers to distribute traffic across multiple endpoints.
- Use multiple availability zones to mitigate against failure.
- Use multiple VMs.
- Use higher performance disk tiers.
- Split servers across update domains to prevent disruption owing to Microsoft patching.
- Split servers across fault domains for maximum resilience.

These are just some of the options available for maximum availability, but since all Azure services have separate Microsoft SLAs, you would need to multiply all the component SLAs together to arrive at a composite SLA for the whole Azure stack.

Building redundant systems and services is the route to very high availability, but also comes at a significant cost if you choose to duplicate most or all systems and services. Regardless of that, real-world achievement of performance targets of above 99.99% are very difficult to achieve since that only permits a minute of downtime per week!

The Azure Service Lifecycle

The Azure Service Lifecycle defines how every Azure service is presented for public consumption. Every Azure service follows this path:

- Development: Microsoft identify requirements and build the service.
- Public Preview: The service is released for public use, often without much warranty. Consumers can offer feedback to help develop the product or service.
- General Availability (GA): Once an Azure service has been validated and tested, it is released as a production-ready service for all customers.

New features of exiting services follow the same path, so you may see features in preview for a service you use in production. These are available for your use, but be sure to note any service limitations as well as acknowledging the enhancement in preview may be withdrawn.

And I'm sure you'll be relieved to hear that brings the material you will need to pass the exam to a close. Find out about the exam itself next!

Good Luck!

The Exam when I took it had just been updated and featured 55 questions – mostly multiple choice with a few drag and drop 'put the required operations in the right order' type questions.

It was an 85-minute exam, it took me around half that time. You need a score of 700/1000 to pass, which a solid grasp of the material in this book should easily get you!

The contents of this book, plus a familiarity with the Azure Portal, were all I needed to pass AZ-900 and become Microsoft Certified on Azure Fundamentals!

Contacting the Author

If you have any comments on this book, questions for me or suggestions for the next edition you can contact me at the following address:

publications@blackchili.co.uk.

You will find my professional profile on LinkedIn here:

https://www.linkedin.com/in/renhimself/

Made in the USA
Middletown, DE
02 September 2021